I Survived
Didn't I?

I Survived Didn't I?

THE GREAT WAR REMINISCENCES OF PRIVATE 'GINGER' BRYNE

Edited & Introduced by
JOY M. CAVE

Pen & Sword
MILITARY

First published in 1993 by Leo Cooper
And reprinted in 2014 by
PEN & SWORD MILITARY
An imprint of
Pen & Sword Books Ltd
47 Church Street
Barnsley, South Yorkshire
S70 2AS

ISBN 978 1 47382 124 8

Printed and bound in England
By CPI Group (UK) Ltd, Croydon, CR0 4YY

Pen & Sword Books Ltd incorporates the Imprints of Aviation, Atlas,
Family History, Fiction, Maritime, Military, Discovery, Politics, History,
Archaeology, Select, Wharncliffe Local History, Wharncliffe True Crime,
Military Classics, Wharncliffe Transport, Leo Cooper, The Praetorian Press,
Remember When, Seaforth Publishing and Frontline Publishing

For a complete list of Pen & Sword titles please contact
PEN & SWORD BOOKS LIMITED
47 Church Street, Barnsley, South Yorkshire, S70 2AS, England
E-mail: enquiries@pen-and-sword.co.uk
Website: www.pen-and-sword.co.uk

CONTENTS

ILLUSTRATIONS

MAPS

ACKNOWLEDGEMENTS

The editor would like to express most sincere thanks to the late Mr John Giles; to Miss Sue Cox for permission to include her poem, 'The Return'; to Mr Richard Dunning for permission to reproduce the photograph of Mr Byrne at Beaumont-Hamel in 1978; and to Mr Ron Burns for his help with the last chapter, 'Sixty-Two Years Later'.

To my husband my affectionate thanks for so much: for the immensely detailed work involved in transcribing the original tape-recordings, for constructive criticism on many important points, for support and encouragement at all times, but especially for the hours of painstaking care that produced the sketch maps so necessary to a work of this kind.

Special thanks go to Mr Byrne's son, Charlie Byrne Junior. Old Mr Byrne himself read and amended the original typed draft but, after his sudden death, 'Young Charlie' put aside his natural grief and distress in order to read through and approve the final draft. There was a great affection and understanding between him and his father and no one knew better the exact expression that would conform to 'Old Charlie's' wishes. My husband and I are delighted to count him and his wife, Sue, as friends. There are times when he reminds us of his father. And that is high praise.

JOY CAVE

FOREWORD

In 1977, my friend Malcolm Brown rang me up to tell me that he had been interviewing old soldiers for a BBC programme and thought there was one I should find interesting because 'he went over the top with your Newfoundlanders'.

I duly made my way to Sandridge in Hertfordshire and knocked on Charlie Byrne's door. I was made very welcome. Over at least half a dozen week-ends and numerous cups of tea Charlie talked and my tape-recorder rolled. Periodically it had to be stopped because Charlie's little dog, Peggy, insisted on getting in on the act. It also had to be silenced occasionally because the old man's memories overwhelmed him — particularly those concerning Beaumont-Hamel — and tears came into his eyes.

'You know,' he said to me at one point, 'it's funny really: I can remember that day, 1st July, 1916, as though it was yesterday; but I can't remember whether I paid the milkman last week!'

Although our subject was so serious — indeed tragic — there was much laughter, not only in those interviews, but during our adjournments to Charlie's local.

I much regret that this gallant old soldier died before the book was completed. My husband and I miss his company still. It was a great privilege to have known him.

Chapter 1

Son of a Gun

'Oh, I'm the son, the son of a gun
The son of a gambolier.
Come all you gay young fellows
That drink your whisky clear,
I'm a rolling rag of poverty,
I'm a bloody old Engineer.'

(Old Army song – source unknown.)

A complete analysis of precisely why and how the First World War broke out is not essential to this narrative. It is certain that Charlie Byrne did not understand why it happened. It was enough for him that it did happen. Like most of the young men of his time he rushed off to join the colours, impelled by a complex of emotions that he does not stop to explain and which he probably could not have explained even to himself. One day he heard a military band playing as it marched down the street and to use his own words: 'I thought to myself, Blow this! I'm off,' and off he went.

My daughter once asked Old Charlie why he had joined up. He scratched his head. 'I dunno, ducks,' he said ruefully, 'And that's the truth. I just don't really know. But,' he added proudly, 'I wouldn't have missed it, you know, not for anything.' Pressed still further he attempted to fit his individual destiny (so typical of many millions) into the greater European pattern by stating firmly, 'The Kaiser started it, you know. That's what really done it' – which is edging closer to the reality as people then understood it. Chuckling, he then went on: 'Did you ever hear the story about how an old soldier told General Haig who started the war? Well, he was a quiet man, Haig, not a chatty sort, not a lot to say for 'isself. One day he was inspecting a body of troops, going up and down the lines of men, see. And he stops in front of one old soldier who'd got a row of medals up – old Regular he was. General Haig apparently decides he'll have a friendly word with 'im. "Where did you start the war?" he says. The old soldier looks at 'im for a second or two, then he says – very polite, "I didn't start it, Sir. I always thought the Kaiser did that." '

Whoever started it, whatever started it, the outcome was to send Charlie Byrne and millions like him into the armies of Europe.

But before he went to the Western Front, brief mention must be made of the tragic 'side-show' in Turkey. This did not quite involve Charlie himself but it engulfed his elder brother. In 1915 the British decided that battering on Europe's front door into Germany (the Western Front) was fruitless, so an attack on the back door through Turkey was decided upon. The Gallipoli Campaign was brilliantly conceived, but it failed and cost the lives of brother Jim and about thirty-eight thousand other British and Empire soldiers.

Private James Byrne was killed on 4 June 1915. On that day 88 Brigade of the 29th Division, in which his battalion was serving, attacked the Turkish positions between the Gully and Krithia Nullah. The attack was unsuccessful. The names of the casualties of the Hampshire Regiment who have no known graves on the Gallipoli Peninsula are inscribed on ten panels (nos. 125 to 134) of the Helles Memorial which is on the south-western tip of the Peninsula, between Tekke Burnu and Sedd el Bahr. The name of 7698 Private James Byrne, age 26, is among them.

On the early morning of 9 January 1916, all British troops were withdrawn from the Peninsula. The decision to evacuate was taken by the Government in early December 1915. Young Charlie Byrne of the 2nd Battalion, the Hampshire Regiment, embarked for the Middle East on 21 November so it is likely that his draft was earmarked as replacements for the sadly depleted

2nd Battalion. Fortunately for him the troopship went to Egypt instead.

I'm a soldier's son all right. But I was a machine-gunner, not an Engineer like it says in the song. As to being 'a rolling rag of poverty' — well, we weren't very well off and that's the truth.

My father, Daniel, was a private in the Hampshire Regiment. Smart man he was, with a ginger moustache. He enlisted on 5 May 1881, and his regimental number was 1936. I was born on 21 November 1896, in Dublin, when he was stationed at Richmond Barracks. There were eight of us in the family — Jim, Cissie, Steve, Mary, Patsy, Lena and Danny (the baby) and me. I was the fourth child. Everywhere the Regiment was moved about Mum had a baby: we were born all over the place. Jim was born in Chatham, I think, and so was my eldest sister; Stevie and Mary were born in Cork and Danny in St Margaret's Hospital when we were living in Thornhill Road in Aldershot. Like I said, I was born in Dublin so that made me an Irishman, a Mick — gave me a bit of trouble later on in life when I applied for a passport, but that's another story.

Mother died in 1908, when Danny was about two-and-a-half years old. Dad finished with the army in the early 1900s — I'd be about seven then — and got a job as a labourer at Aldershot. His money was 17s.6d. a week: he'd a family of us to keep on that and his bit of an army pension. He'd served with the colours 22 years 201 days: for that his pension was £5.2s.9d. a quarter. If you work that out it's 1s.1½d. per day. I've been with him to Aldershot Post Office to see him draw it: five gold sovereigns and the odd change. That's what we had to live on for three months; still that's how it was in those days. He served in the Burma War and the South African War and had medals but we had to pawn those at odd times. He died in 1917 while I was in France in the Great

War and he's buried in the Military Cemetery at Aldershot.

I left school when I was twelve. I went to the RE and ASC School: the Army School near Stanhope Lines in Aldershot. Barrack Rats they used to call us. Very strict they were with us kids but we got a good elementary education even if they were inclined to jog your memory with an ebony ruler.

I had a few odd jobs; then I was apprenticed to a blacksmith as a striker – I used to use a big hammer all day long. When the war broke out I was seventeen years and eight months old. One day I saw the band go by and I thought to myself, Blow this! I'm off. So I went back to the two rooms where we lived and took my overalls off, and away I went down to the station for Winchester. When I got there and I was going through the barrier the ticket-collector said, 'Hullo, mate. Where you going, then?'

I said, 'To join the Hampshires.'

'Good luck to you, young feller-me-lad,' he says.

I got down to the guard-room and I said to the Sergeant, 'I've come to join the Regiment.'

'Very good,' he replied and told me to go to a hut round the cook-house and offered to show me the way. I laughed and told him not to bother. I knew my way – Dad had been on the Depot for odd spells.

So I went in this big hut and instead of there being one recruiting sergeant there was about a dozen; all sitting behind army tables with blankets on top. This was August 1914 and there was such a rush to join up, there were a lot of men called Section D men, Reservists, who were being called up, plus us fellows who wanted to volunteer. We sat on a big form and were called to the tables one by one. When my turn came the Sergeant didn't look up, he just said, 'Sit down. Name?'

'Byrne,' I said.

Then he looked up. 'How do you spell it?' So I spells

it for him.

'Where were you born?'

'In Dublin.'

'What was your father?'

'A soldier.'

So he says, 'What year were you born?'

'Round about early 1895.' (I had to put my age up a bit, see, because they wouldn't take you under nineteen).

'Where's your birth certificate then?'

That threw me for a second, but I comes back quick, 'I haven't got it.'

'You got a brother called James?'

'Yes.'

'Was your father's name Daniel Byrne?'

'Yes.' I began to wonder what was going on.

'Is he still alive?'

'Yes, he's in the Works Department at Aldershot.'

So he puts his pen down, still looking straight at me and he says, 'Do you know who you're talking to?'

'No.'

'You're talking to your bloody godfather, that's who. I'm Sergeant Duffey I am. I was godfather to your Dad's children and he stood godfather to mine. How old do you reckon you are, then?'

'Nineteen.'

'Oh no, you're not! I'll tell you how old you are 'cos I know when the Hampshires were stationed in Dublin. You're only eighteen.'

I thought to myself, Just my luck. Of course I didn't recognize him − I hadn't seen him since I was a baby.

'No,' he went on, 'you're not even that. You're only about seventeen and eight or nine months.'

'Can't you swing it for me?'

'No,' he says, very stern. But he was smiling. 'Got your father's red hair, I see,' he says. 'Only one of the boys to have his red hair.'

Anyway, after a bit of hoo-ha they let me in; put me

in the Special Reserves for six months. But the war had started so I knew I'd be in all the way through, because you went in for what they called 'the duration' then. Not that we knew then how long it was going to be. I thought I might miss it all. There's a laugh!

So I got my equipment at Winchester. I knew how to put it all together and how to lay it out for inspection. Lot of blokes there didn't know what went where. I knew what all the bloomin' bugle calls meant too. And I knew the old cook as well − old Wobbly Ford. He was called Wobbly because he was a big fat bloke. It can be a very good thing to be on friendly terms with an army cook.

I got along all right, and when they sent me to Gosport and I'd trained as a machine-gunner I had a bright idea − I'd pull a fast one. I altered the seven on my papers to a nine, making me nineteen on enlistment. I got with some blokes who was home on a draft from India. They were going to Warwickshire. Eventually − about March 1915 − they embarked at Avonmouth: two companies went on the HMT *Aragon* and two on the *Manitou*. When they got to Tenedos two companies went on the *River Clyde*. I expect you've heard about the *River Clyde* at Gallipoli? But I didn't go. My family connections was about to catch up with me.

My brother Steve, No. 8507 he was, played the drums in the Corps of Drums. And there he was playing the drums when we got there. I spotted him and he spotted me standing there; so when they fell out he comes stumping over to me − he was a little short fellow; a bit chubby. 'What are you doing here then?' he says.

'What do you think I'm doing? I'm in the Second Hampshires.'

'Oh!' he says. 'Oh! You wait till our Jim hears about this.'

At this moment our eldest brother, Jim − fine, smart fellow with a moustache − he'd seen the two of us talking together; he come over to find out what it was all about. He didn't know about me because he was in a different Company you see, and I'd been away doing my course on machine-guns.

'You're not going,' he said straightaway. 'I'll see to that. Two of us is enough.'

Next day I got sent for by Colonel Carrington-Smith. He'd got my papers on the table in front of him. '4124, Private Byrne, C.,' he says. 'Your brother tells me that you're not nineteen yet.'

'Well, if he says so, he must be right, Sir.'

'Are you nineteen or not? I want the truth.'

'No, Sir, I'm not, but I'd like to go to the battalion.'

'That you shall do,' he says flat out, 'when you're old enough.'

So I got sent back to Gosport. Jim went to Gallipoli with the draft. They landed on 25th April and Jim was killed on 4th June. So I suppose if I'd wangled to go my number might have been up too because the Hampshires got knocked about something cruel round Gully Ravine.

I finally sailed on my nineteenth birthday: 21st November 1915. I forget now where we was supposed to be making for, but the ship in front of us, the *Royal Edward* got torpedoed in the Aegean Sea. Lot of troops went down with that ship.

We were disembarked at Alexandria; then we went down to Suez and Ismalia and then back up to Alex again. I dunno what we were supposed to be doing, I'm sure. Very hot and dusty it was – all sandy desert round that way.

I first saw the Newfoundlanders in Egypt: they were a grand bunch, and I was to get mixed up with them in a queer sort of way before many months was out. But, anyway, after traipsing up and down the desert in an aimless sort of way – nobody never told you nothing in them days – we embarked again and off we went: to France this time.

Chapter 2

May 1916

'What did you join the Army for?
Why did you join the Army?
What did you join the Army for?
You must have been bloody well barmy.'

(1914-1918 Song. Sung to the tune of 'Here's to the
Maiden of Bashful Fifteen')

When Private Byrne disembarked from the *Transylvania* at Marseilles on 20 March, 1916, he was part of the build-up for the 'Big Push' which would come to be known as the Battle of the Somme. At that time he was blissfully unaware of that fact.

The 29th Division arrived in the Louvencourt area at the end of May. The sector which was the particular concern of the 88 Brigade (of which the 2nd Battalion the Hampshire Regiment and the 1st Battalion the Newfoundland Regiment formed part) extended from a little north of the sunken road between Auchonvillers and Beaumont-Hamel to a point about half a mile from the village of Hamel in the valley of the Ancre.

At that time it was regarded as a 'quiet' sector. 'Mr Boche ain't a bad feller. You leave 'im alone: 'e'll leave you alone,' commented one NCO of the garrison of a front-line trench from whom one unit took over in April.

But the tremendous preparations required for the battle ahead — a largely British affair planned to relieve pressure on the French at Verdun — were difficult to keep secret and anyhow there seem to have been few attempts to observe even elementary security precautions. The coming attack was openly discussed in London drawing-rooms. German espionage and German Intelligence were in no doubt about the imminent offensive and where it was to occur.

Meantime the units in the trenches above the Somme existed in the normal fashion of Great War soldiering. They did tours of trench duty, provided working and wiring parties, went out on patrols, and did training exercises; some of them got killed and many more were seriously injured. Young Private Byrne went his cheerful way, always 'obeying the last order' as he puts it. He had some interesting – and frightening – experiences.

But the 29th Division was not composed of 'green' troops. Apart from the Newfoundlanders, the units were experienced Regular Army men and they knew the score. This division had missed the earlier 1914 battles that had taken such a toll of other formations. They observed the activities going on around them – guns moving, masses of dumps of stores and many other things – and shook their heads. Obviously it was not going to be 'quiet' on their sector for long: the stage was being set for 'a most unholy dust-up.'

I was a bit unfortunate in that I was the only man in my platoon who hadn't been to India and that made me sort of odd man out. They weren't unkind to me but I might as well not have been there. They used to talk among themselves using a lot of Hindustani words they'd picked up in India. I understood most of what they were saying because I'd picked up a lot of this Army Hindustani from my Dad, but I didn't let on. I just kept quiet, did as I was told, kept my head down and kept my nose clean. I grew a thick skin and I didn't get fed up. Except for the Corporal, that is. He didn't like me at all and he wanted to be rid of me. I'd got red hair and he didn't like that: but worse than that, I'd got a terrible stutter as a young man. I almost completely got over it as I got older; funny thing was I think the war helped me to get over it. But

WESTERN FRONT 1916-18

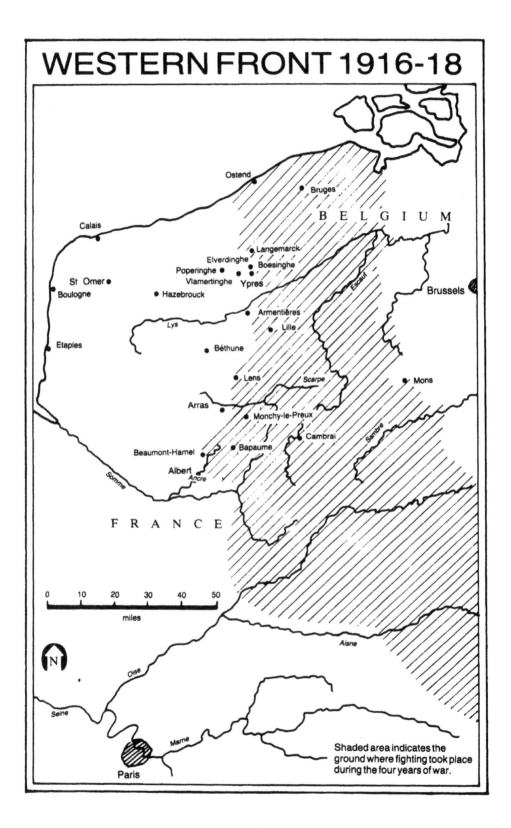

Ostend

Bruges

B E L G I U M

Calais

Langemarck
Elverdinghe
Poperinghe ● Boesinghe
St Omer ● Vlamertinghe ● Ypres
Boulogne Hazebrouck

Brussels

Armentières
Lys Lille

Etaples Béthune

Lens Scarpe Mons

Arras
Monchy-le-Preux

Escaut

Sambre

Beaumont-Hamel Bapaume Cambrai
Albert Ancre
Somme

F R A N C E

0 10 20 30 40 50
miles

N

Oise
Aisne

Seine
Marne

Paris

Shaded area indicates the
ground where fighting took place
during the four years of war.

this Corporal used to think I was sub-normal or mentally backward or something. I knew I wasn't that thick or stupid but it wasn't easy to keep cheerful when that Corporal was about. I could take it all right, but I used to get every bloomin' fatigue that was going — emptying sanitary pails, digging trenches, wiring parties. Wiring parties! At one time I got to thinking I'd put most of the wire up on our part of the Western Front all by meself! You'll hear more about that Corporal later. He came to a no good end up in the Salient: not that I was glad about it in the end — I wasn't.

Anyways we crawled up from Marseilles to a place whose name I forget — near Albert it was — in one of those French troop trains. It said on the wagon, in French of course, that there was room for eight horses or forty men. I don't know how the eight horses got on but it was a tight fit for forty blokes with all their equipment. Nor they didn't travel at what you may call express speed neither. But we got there in the end. Then off we march to a little village called Louvencourt. It wasn't far behind the front line but it wasn't much knocked about — not then. The civilians were still living there. There was the Hampshires and the Newfoundlanders billeted there.

We must have got there about the end of May 1916. We did ten days in the line, then ten days out of it, and we did two spells in the line before July 1st.

The first time in the line wasn't too bad — nice and quiet, comparatively speaking.

By accident I had quite an interesting experience during that first tour. We'd been in this trench about four days. It was after evening 'Stand-to.' In the trenches there wasn't much time for what you normally do in peacetime — sleep, that is. Everyone on both sides was very busy at night; digging, mending trenches, and wiring. You mostly got your kip during the day as and when you got the opportunity. But there were two periods of the day that were reckoned particularly dangerous and that was at dawn and at dusk: because that was the most likely time for trench raids and other little nastinesses. So we had morning and evening 'Stand-to' when everyone was alerted and lined up, and sentries posted, and officers scurrying here and there and what not.

Anyway, just after 'Stand-to' on this particular evening up comes my friend the Corporal and he snaps at me: 'Put your rifle over there and take a couple of pineapples' — by that he meant two Mills bombs — 'and accompany this officer.'

I'd never seen this officer before. He had a maple leaf on his collar. He was a Canadian but he was attached to the Hampshires. I found out later his name was Lieutenant Morley but he didn't say anything to me that first time, just went off up the trench with me going after him. Then he turned down a little sap there was. A sap is a narrow trench that goes outwards from the main front line into No Man's Land. This particular sap had three blokes in it at the bottom and the sap ended about four yards from a sunken road which was out in No Man's Land. The officer stopped to have a word with these three men: told them we was going out, I suppose, and not to shoot at us when we was coming back. But I didn't hear what he said to them — as you may suppose he wasn't shouting because we weren't that far off the German front lines — and he never said a word to me; didn't even ask me who I was. I reckon he thought that ignorant Corporal of mine had given me the full strength, but he hadn't of course.

So we left the three blokes behind and went crawling the rest of the way up this sap on our hands and knees. When we got to the end, bless my soul if he didn't pop out over the top and went right into No Man's Land. I thought he'd gone barmy but my orders was to follow him, so I followed him.

I wonder where I'm off to? I thought to myself. He can't be going to call on those Saxons opposite for a friendly chit-chat. The natives in them parts are what is known as hostile. Nor we can't be a raiding party because there's only two of us. This could be bloody dangerous!

After a little while he disappeared in the dark in front of me and I find we're in a sunken road. Then I realized. There was one of these sunken roads that started from behind our trenches and went towards the Germans, then it took a sort of right-hand bend and went almost parallel with their front line for a bit. As a matter of fact the German wire was only about eighteen inches above your head at one point. It was just deep enough so that you could crawl along it in the dark and you wouldn't be seen because you were below the surface of the ground. When we first got into the sunken road he put his mouth right by my ear and whispered, 'We're going a bit further on, then I shall stop and give you my watch. You stand fast. Then if I'm not back in a quarter of an hour, you go back to the sap.' I nodded my head. We crawled on a bit further. I counted up to about ninety-four crawling paces (if you get my meaning), then he stopped. He took his watch off, put it on my left arm, pointed to the time on the luminous dial and off he went.

I was pretty comfortable in that sunken road. One or two shells went over and the odd trench mortar, but you were quite safe in the middle. No one wastes ammunition on No Man's Land in the ordinary course of things. I was probably safer there than I was in my own trench. Anyway, the last order I'd had was to stay put where I was for quarter of an hour so I laid easy and put I stayed.

He was back just inside the quarter hour, gives me a dig in the ribs and off we goes back again. I counted my paces, out of the sunken road, find the sap, down into it, back to the trench. He took the watch back and I went back to my Company. Nothing to it. Good job done. Mind, what the job was, I'd no idea. I found out later. I'd been on what was called a listening patrol. Exactly what Lieutenant Morley was listening for I never did find out. He must have had good ears or maybe he had some kind of listening device. *I* dunno, and no one ever told me. You didn't ask questions in those days. I had my orders. That had to be good enough for me.

The following night round he came again. I thought, Hullo! Someone's for it tonight. Down that sunken road. It was me. The Corporal said, 'Come on you. You know what to do. Leave your rifle. Collect a couple of bombs.'

We'd just got down into the sap and he stopped for a little while.

'What's your name?' he asked.

'Charlie.'

'Charlie what?'

'Charlie Byrne — B-Y-R-N-E.'

'Oh, ah!' he said. 'And how old are you?'

'Nineteen.'

'What were you in civilian life?'

'I'd just started work as a blacksmith's striker, but being as the war broke out and as I was born in the army, I thought I'd join up.'

'Born in the army, eh!' he said. 'That's interesting. I'm from Canada: Ottawa. I was a private detective in civilian life.'

'Better bloomin' job than me.'

He laughed and looked at his watch. 'Well, we've both got a difficult job now,' he said, 'and we'd better be getting on with it. Time we buzzed off.'

So off we buzzed. Same instructions as before. But this time things didn't go so smoothly. He went over his time. I waited and I waited, but he didn't come back. Jerry was a bit fidgety, too. There were quite a few shells dropping over the lines towards where the artillery was and there was star shells and Very lights. He was having a right go. I thought there was going to be an attack or something. I didn't need the luminous dial on that watch: both sides were sending up Very lights — it was almost like bloomin' day-time.

I thought to myself, Where the hell's he got to! I'll have to go back. Always obey the last order, come what may. But I dunno. I can't just leave him. Suppose he's got a bit of shrapnel in his leg or something and he can't move? So I done the wrong thing. I made my way after him, crawling nearer to the German line. That's when I found out the German wire was only eighteen inches above my head, so you can see how close the Germans were. He'd gone further down still so he must almost have got right up to their line. He must have been bloomin' batty, but he had some courage, you know. Goodness knows what he got up to down there.

Just as I began to wonder what I ought to do next I met him head-on. He pushed me, much as to say, Get back where I told you. I started back, and in my hurry I forgot how many paces I'd gone over the ninety-eight I'd counted from where we originally started. I did something I didn't often do in the War — I lost meself. I was very proud of my bump of direction; I was noted for it. 'You go with Ginger,' they used to say, 'Ginge don't get lost.' Nor I didn't either. I don't know why. I used to notice things on my way to somewhere — bit of discarded equipment, a dead mule with his legs sticking one way or a funny-shaped hole or a corkscrew support blown to a queer angle, and things like that. And I'd remember and find my way back by them.

But I was lost this time and no mistake. I counted my original ninety-eight paces and then added on what I thought was the right number and then I stopped and got out of the sunken road and crawled towards where I thought the sap was; but it wasn't. Fortunately everything had quietened down again and there were no lights going up.

'Where's the sap?' the officer hisses at me.

'Must be round here somewhere,' I whispers back. I

was in a right pickle. Anyway the three blokes who were on guard in the deepest part of the sap must have been looking out for us as we were overdue. Luckily they weren't feeling trigger-happy or that would have been that. But just as I was feeling a bit desperate I heard, 'Tsst, tsst − over here.' And we tumbled thankfully into the sap.

We went back up to the main trench, me plodding along behind him. He took his watch back off me. 'Next time, do what you're told to do,' he said sharpish, and walked away.

'Blimey,' I thought, 'I'm in the cart here.' So I followed him along till we got to the traverse where I'd started from and I touched him on the shoulder and he stopped. 'I'm sorry, Sir,' I stammered (terrible stammer I had then), 'I'm sorry I disobeyed orders. But I thought you might have been in trouble.'

He paused for a while and then grinned. 'Damn nearly was,' he said: 'I suppose I'd have done the same thing myself under similar circumstances. That's all right. Come and see me when you get back to Louvencourt.'

Funny thing − although we were in the line for quite a few days after that I didn't see him again. Not in the line. But I did go back to see him and he was a real friend to me: indirectly saved my life in a queer sort of way.

The rest of the time in the line was fairly routine. We had a Saxon lot opposite us and they didn't go looking for trouble. There seemed to be an unwritten law that if one side didn't start no trouble then the other side wouldn't; especially at night when everyone was busy. It was lovely really. Down behind Beaumont-Hamel, if the wind was in the right direction, you could hear the old German limbers going over the cobblestones and our blokes would be coming up from Englebelmer with our rations on the limbers. Jerry was knocking in the posts to put the wire up. We'd be doing the same. Nobody would be sounding off at anybody else. General lack of what the high-ups with red tabs would call offensive spirit. You could put up with the war under those circumstances. There was one fellow in the German lines who used to play the cornet lovely. Sometimes he used to play English tunes. You should have heard him playing 'Home, Sweet Home'. But when we went out of the line the mob that relieved us — South Wales Borderers I think it was — went out on a trench raid and captured the bloody cornet and all. I never actually saw it, but that's the way the story went: and certainly when we went in next time I never heard it no more.

That first time in the line was reasonably quiet, taking things by and large, except for one night. I'll never forget it. I was lucky. I wasn't out wiring that night; I'd been out the night previous so I was off. It was the second last day of our ten days in. Our wiring party was out. Jerry was wiring, just to our left — I could hear him plain as anything. Then past me comes trotting four machine-gunners. Not ours. Don't know where they come from. I wasn't on the machine-guns then, though I'd been trained. I was an ordinary rifleman in those days. They went down the trench with the old tripod and machine-gun and blokes were saying, 'Wonder where they're off to?' They went down about five bays past us, set up and then began blasting off. They opened up on the Jerry wiring party. They must have sent a couple of belts through before Jerry started answering back. Then he answered all right — just where our wiring party was. He mowed them down. Then our eighteen-pounders started. Then Jerry's big guns started. Everybody was knocking hell out of everything for a bit. Then these blokes takes the pins out, folds up the tripod and they're a hundred-and-fifty yards up the trench and out of the way when the party really got going and we were left taking the can back. They didn't half get cussed — trigger-happy was the only polite word that was said about them. They must have had orders. But what did they want to go and do a thing like that for? Making everybody nasty-tempered. But, apart from that bit of nonsense, that first tour wasn't bad and we duly got relieved and went out of the line.

But when we come out of the line we didn't get a holiday or a rest period or anything of that kind. The Newfoundlanders and the Hampshires were stuck out in the fields every day. They got us round in circles, each company in a circle, and we had training exercises. Then the Sergeant would give us instruction. As I remember, it went something like this:

'Now, when the bombardment opens, it will be so intense that when it's finished the German line will be totally disintegrated.' (Disintegrated — that's the word they used: *I* never heard the word before; don't suppose most of the blokes knew what it meant). 'The wire will be all blown away and you will outnumber the Germans three to one. As soon as the whistle goes, you've got to mount the parapet and there'll be gaps cut in the wire for you to go through.'

I don't know which poor devils had cut the gaps in the wire, because it was them that was in the trenches while we was at rest. Cutting gaps in wire is no easy job; you have to do it in the dark and if the flares go up there's Jerry popping off at you. Wiring is no fun at all and cutting it is even worse. 'When you've gone through the gaps in the wire,' he says, 'you walk out into No Man's Land. You must walk. No man is to run because you might run into our own defensive barrage. Any man getting killed or wounded by our own barrage will be liable to court-martial.' (I had to laugh at this.) 'Now when you get to the second line you stop there until reinforcements come up and then you go forward and take the next line. Now, does every man understand? All right then. Extended order!'

So we got into extended order and there we was trampling down all the corn the poor old farmer had growing in this big field; ruining his crops we were. 'Now,' said the Sergeant, 'now the bombardment's on. Everybody walk at the high port.' (That's a drill term — it means you carry your rifle in your two hands in front of you, across your body.) 'Don't run, you: you're too far in front. Keep your dressing. Now you're in the second line. Stop and wait for your reinforcements. The reinforcements are coming. They won't be long. Now they're here. When the whistle blows, charge to take the next line. Now!'

Of course it was ridiculous, you know. There we were shouting 'Charge' and dashing across the field with our bloody bayonets. We felt silly. I can't remember whether it was raining or not. I don't think it was. Though, as I remember it, June 1916 wasn't a very nice month. There was a lot of rain.

We went into the line for our second tour. This time things were a bit naughty. The fellers I was with, being old soldiers and having been out to India and knowing everything there was to know, began to notice things. They noticed the heavy guns going up and our bombardment getting heavier and other things too. And they shook their heads. 'Trouble brewin',' they said. I was young and foolish and I wasn't taking much notice: they were always talking among themselves and letting on they knew such a lot. Mind, they were right this time, though. But I was given orders and I obeyed them. I follered the feller in front of me and that was about my limit. You weren't exactly encouraged to let your imagination run riot or use your initiative or anything like that in those days. Dear me, no.

One night while we were in the line I was on guard down that sap — the one that was so important to me when I was out on the listening patrol with Lieutenant Morley — and we heard a noise. Now that was queer because you'd be told if there was anybody coming in; if there was any patrols out. So I looks round the corner of the traverse and I said to the Corporal, 'Who's this coming down then?'

'Get out of the way,' he said (in his usual polite fashion) and he takes a quick look. 'It's a bloody Jerry, that's who,' he said. 'He's got a Jerry hat on. Stand back. Don't make a noise.' So I stood back, and when this feller came round the corner of the traverse the old Corporal gave him a right bloody thump. Talk about Cassius Clay. Knocked him right out, flat on his back, poor little devil. Blond young lad he was, didn't look much above seventeen. He had no rifle. Don't know what he was doing. Maybe he'd done what I nearly did and lost himself – easy enough in the dark. So he ditched everything and tried to make his way back light in case he had to run for it. Probably thought he was getting back into his own trench; one sap looks much like another in the dark. Poor little chap. He didn't have no bombs in his pockets – just his watch and some letters and photographs. He was all right when he come round from the Corporal's thump. No rifle, no bombs, no equipment, no bayonet: he was no bother. We kept him there till we went back in the morning and we give him to the Interrogating Officer. Don't know what happened to him. Poor little Jerry – lost hisself, that's what. Still, he was happy. His war was over.

On the fourth day in I think it was, we get put in the support trench. Not that that made a lot of difference, because it was only about twenty-five yards or so back from the front line: except I suppose you'd got the comfortable thought that there was someone in front of you and you wouldn't be worried with trench raids and things of that kind. One night me and another feller got sent back to the rendezvous to pick up some rations. The rendezvous was on the road from Englebelmer and the limbers used to come up there, unload their stuff and take back the empty petrol cans. We had to take two empty petrol cans each because if you didn't you wouldn't get any water. It tasted of petrol a bit but it was better than water out of shell-holes. We was given a big dixie full of stew and we'd just started back when Jerry opens up. Somebody somewhere must have upset him. He was knocking hell out of this road. We got in a communication trench called Constitution Hill and the feller behind me says, 'Drop it, Ginge. Let's stop here for a while. It's a bit unhealthy round here.' So we stopped there for a while but Jerry was still throwing things about; knocking hell out of the place. I said, 'We've got to get up there. We've got the rations. No doubt about it. We've got to go.' So we went. We had a hell of a job getting this blinking dixie full of stew round the traverses. There was a lot of bangs and stuff flying about. We kept dropping the dixie in the mud. By the time we got there the stew was almost cold. But, as I said, they was bloody lucky to get any stew at all that night.

That was the night I lost my only real mate – old Ted Smith. He was two traverses up from me. Jerry was still having a good old go. Hellish row there was. Someone tells me Ted has stopped one, so I went to see. He was two years older than me and he'd been right through the Gallipoli campaign. When I got there he'd got one arm round the stretcher-bearer's neck but one side of him was a horrible sight. He was still conscious. 'Look wot they done to me, Ginge,' he says. 'Look wot they done to me.' It was a terrible sight. Anyway he lived. His left arm was completely gone. I went to the hospital to see him when I was on leave. They gave him a job delivering letters. He still had his right arm, see. He used to play dominoes. But I missed old Ted.

We came out of the line after that lot and we did some more of this training I was telling you about. Then one day they marched us down by companies to a farm at the bottom of Louvencourt and there was this old farmer with a big whetstone. You got your bayonet out, give it to the old French farmer and you wind the handle while he puts a bloody sharp point on it. When it was finished you could shave yourself with it. When we got back to the billets the Sergeant told us to put our equipment together and you could hear the old barrack-room lawyers (that was what I called these know-alls from India) saying, 'By Christ, there's going to be some fireworks soon.' One bloke said, 'That's all right. You've only had your bayonets sharpened to make bloody toast with. Everybody will be going home because the bloody war will be over in three weeks' time. So don't let it worry you.' I just listened. I didn't know what to think. I supposed they knew better than me. They was older and Regular soldiers an' all.

There was about one in five or six men kitted out with three-cornered tin discs on their haversacks. This was so our aeroplanes could tell us from the Jerries and see how far we'd got. There was also about one in four or five of us that had a pair of wire-cutters stuck on the end of the rifle. They come out like horns. If the barbed wire was strung tight you'd push against it with these things and it would part with a twang. But if the wire was loose you'd push agin it and keep on pushing till you were blue − or till Jerry picked you off − but they wouldn't work. Just my luck! You can bet your life young Charlie got kitted up with a pair of these bloody wire-cutters.

The next day we had a day off. Nobody did anything. Everybody was merry and bright. We all had a nice drink in the estaminet and blokes was writing field cards: they didn't say much − just 'I am well', 'I am wounded', 'I am going to the Base for....' So I got one, crossed out all the lines except 'I am well' and sent it home to my sister who lived in Chelsea.

Daytime went on. I wandered down to the transport lines and had a look at the mules. I used to love them little old donkeys − they weren't donkeys, of course, but that's what I used to call them. People say they're cross-grained and awkward, but they're not really: not half as much so as a lot of human beings I've known. Which brings me back to that Corporal of ours.

I walked round the village, past the pump, down the end where the Newfoundlanders were and then back to the billet for tea about half past four. After tea things were a bit dull and we were sitting around in the barn when in comes this bloomin' bullet-headed Corporal.

'Hey, you,' pointing at me, 'put your equipment on. Leave your pack and your canteen. Follow me.'

So off we went, marching down to the other end of Louvencourt where the Newfoundlanders were. He never said a word except 'Stand there' when we got to a barn. Then he disappeared inside. Outside there was a Newfoundland Corporal and he looked at me and smiled.

'How you getting on, mate,' he says.

So I said, 'All right, thanks.' And I thinks to myself, 'What a bloomin' treat. All friendly like.' You never got that in our billets. I don't reckon my Corporal even knew how to smile. And as to asking how I was getting on – no chance.

After a minute or so my Corporal called me into the barn and there was an officer and two senior NCOs. The officer asked me what machine-guns I knew and when I replied, 'The Maxim and the Vickers,' he told the Newfoundland corporal to take me to Sergeant somebody or other and out we went and over to another barn.

When he pushed the barn door open you couldn't see across it for smoke. Blokes were sitting all round – talking, laughing, joking, writing letters, and playing cards. It was a really friendly atmosphere. So the Corporal walked over to where there were about six blokes in a circle playing pontoon. 'Here you are,' he said to the bloke dealing the cards, 'here's your Number One.'

'Right-oh,' he answered and tells me to sit down. They

finished the hand and then he turned to me and said, 'You're to be Number Three. Know what you gotta do?'

I certainly did. Number One fires the gun. Number Two carries the tripod and feeds the belt through. Number Three is the bloomin' pack-horse: he carries the ammo and gets the belts ready to feed through when each beltful is exhausted. The number of men in a gun-team varied according to circumstances and who was available, but every man in a team should be able to handle the gun in case fellers get knocked out. However, when we'd got sorted out they invited me to join in the game of cards and I had a lucky streak − won five or six francs.

A sergeant came in just as it was getting dusk and said, 'Nearly time, boys.' Then he went off, but one of the group said, 'We've got time for another hand.' After that we got our things together and got fell in on the road outside.

The feller who'd been dealing the cards when I first went in said, 'You keep close to me. Don't lose me.'

There was a lot of the old Louvencourt folk standing round − seeing us off as it were. There weren't any young men − just old men and women. We sloped arms, numbered off, and formed fours.

'Right, by the left, quick march.' And we marched out of Louvencourt like proper soldiers should do.

But, as we were swinging along, chests out, I noticed something. Well, I thought to meself, that's cheerful, that is. Right bloody cheerful, that's what. Those people lining the village street, some of them were crying. Tears pouring down their faces.

Chapter 3

The Newfoundlanders and the First Day on the Somme

'The bells of hell go ting-a-ling, for you but not for me.
The little devils sing-a-ling-a-ling, for you but not for me.
O Death, where is thy sting-a-ling-a-ling, where, grave, thy
    victoree?
The bells of hell go ting-a-ling-a-ling,
For you but not for me.'

(Old Army song)

The first day on the Somme has been exhaustively documented. It was, of course, only the opening of the first of twelve officially named overlapping battles which make up the whole Somme offensive and which lasted until the end of November.

But it is mainly the first day that holds the attention. What someone once referred to as 'the glory and the graveyard of Kitchener's Army – those citizen volunteers who, instantly answering the call in 1914, had formed the first national army of Britain'. By the evening of 1 July 1916, some fifty-seven thousand of his fellow citizen-soldiers were either dead, badly hurt or prisoner up and down the eighteen miles or so of French countryside that is always labelled historically 'The Somme'. Actually this is misleading: the Somme marks the southern boundary of the great battles for the British. It is the Ancre stream, a slow brown tributary of the River Somme, that wound its way through the centre of the really important goings-on so long ago.

So far as young Charlie Byrne was concerned, he was most likely unaware of either the Ancre or the Somme as such. His horizon was very limited. He knew Louvencourt, where his billet was. He knew Englebelmer where the dumps and stores were. He knew the communication trenches and the front-line trenches to the right of Auchonvillers. And he knew that the Germans somewhere to the east existed in a village called Beaumont-Hamel.

Charlie was in the rear of the main movement of the battalion because he was in a machine-gun section. As his story makes clear, he had little idea of what was happening, apart from the fact that whatever it was it was very unpleasant. But when he emerged on the slope towards Y Ravine he was in a favourable position to observe the terrible results of what had happened. He makes his own comments on the steadfastness of the Newfoundlanders. They lost 90 per cent of the men actually engaged in that forlorn and hopeless advance.

So we marched out of Louvencourt, all very smart, as it was getting dark. But when we'd gone a little way the officer said, 'March at ease.' We sang a bit. 'Keep the Home Fires Burning' was one I remember. I knew the way because I'd been up twice before, but being as I was with the Newfoundland Regiment I knew we'd be veering to the left, off my usual route, because the Hampshire's bit of line was further on. Sure enough we went to the left across some fields. The first twice I'd been in the line we got there with hardly a shot being fired, but this time they were sending some bloomin' heavy stuff over. Jerry was searching for our guns. He'd got some of our stuff going his way as well, but Jerry was feeling proper argumentative that night so we had really rather a dicey journey for the last part. But I don't remember anybody being wounded or anything like that.

When we got to Englebelmer we looked sharp getting the boxes of ammo. There was blokes grabbing at

BEAUMONT-HAMEL AREA
OF THE SOMME BATTLEFIELD

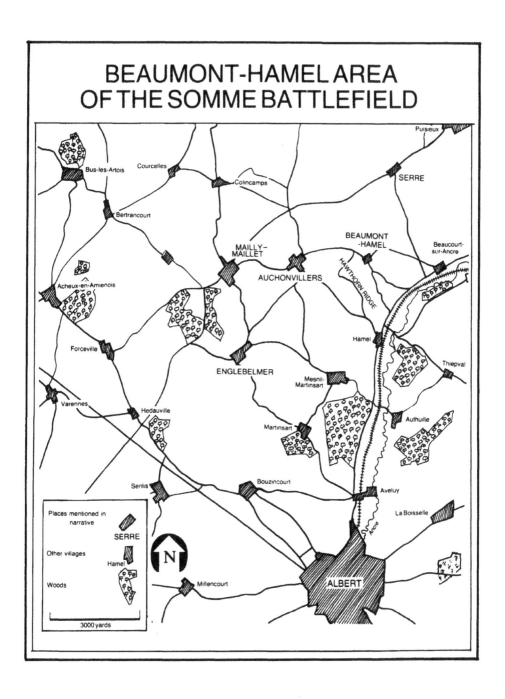

everything and carting them off — duckboards, picks, shovels, and all kinds of things. I kept up with this feller in front, the one who'd said 'Don't lose me', and the three of us marched off together. I must have been in the last five or ten men of the platoon. I don't know how many was behind me.

At any rate we started off up this communication trench — it was narrow and shallow, only three or four foot deep. The further you went, the deeper it got. I'd got a box of ammo in each hand and that accursed rifle. You can't really carry ammunition boxes with a rifle on your shoulder. The rifle kept sliding off and I was dragging it along because I had to keep up with the feller in front. Then we'd have to stop. Then we'd start off again: then stop again. And all the while the trench was getting deeper and deeper and deeper till the order got passed back — 'No smoking'; that meant we were getting near the front line.

I felt sorry for the poor fellers who had to mend the [telephone] wires as there was wires laying about everywhere. The wires were looped on the side of the trench with a sort of wooden bracket: if the wooden peg fell out or someone snagged the wires with a bit of equipment, they'd fall down and blokes walked on them, dragged them all up in a heap, then others would get tangled up and, in the end, it was chaos. I did feel sorry for the signallers who had to sort 'em all out and connect them up — I suppose they were from the field telephones to the guns and various headquarters.

Anyway, we kept going somehow. Then the man in front of me stopped again. 'Is this it?' I asked him.

'I dunno,' he replied.

After a bit, off we go again. We turned up along another trench, round a traverse, on again, round another traverse. Then we stopped again. So I dumped the boxes down again and hiked me rifle up on me shoulder.

'Is this it, then?' I said.

'You keep bloody well saying "Is this it?" every time we stop. 'Ow the 'ell should I know?'

I was a bit rattled. 'Well, *I* don't know how far we've got to go. And are we going in the front line? This is not the front line. There's no fire-steps here, for a start-off.'

'I dunno,' he said again. 'I suppose this might be it.' So he asked the chap in front of him. 'Far as I know, mate,' he says 'this is as far as we go.'

So I thought to meself, 'I'm not going to be mucked about no more with these two bloomin' boxes of ammo and this rifle.' So I took my left puttee off and tied the two boxes together and slung them across one shoulder. And the Number One says, 'Now you're using your 'ead, aren't you? You should have bloomin' well done that afore you started out – not now.'

I thought, He's right. I dunno. I'll never learn. But I didn't say anything. I just sat down on the boxes. A fellow come round with the rum ration. I didn't have any. I was glad later on that I didn't.

All this time the shells were going over, so I thought it was as far as we were going to go for the time being. We had a long, long wait in the dark: seemed hours to me. You could hear our guns were firing from a long way back and the shells were going a long way ahead – big ones. The eighteen-pounders were working away there: it wasn't a big shell but they had a long brass nose-cap – and the blinking din they made! Seemed to slit your ear-drums when they were firing over you: it wasn't so bad if you were behind them. It carried on and on until you got so used to the bombardment that your brain seemed – not asleep exactly – but all boggled with the terrible noise. No one was talking to anyone else because there didn't seem to be anything to say and the din was ferocious.

Then I saw an officer come round the traverse and speak to the Number One. So I says to myself, 'Well, we've got an officer with us, at any rate, with his Sam Browne belt and riding breeches and a little revolver with a cord round his neck.' The rum-jar came round again. I know I was near the end of the row because it wasn't long before he came back again with the rum — so I'd be roughly tenth man from the back.

Things went quiet for a while. Then suddenly the bombardment started up again. It was daylight by then; lovely morning it was. I heard the rattle of machine-gun fire: you could always hear that above everything else. After a while the wounded started coming down: must have been coming up to eight o'clock by then, I suppose, but I'm not sure because I didn't have a watch. The wounded was streaming down in fours and fives, one fellow helping another along; there didn't seem to be any end to them. You got to thinking there couldn't be many left out there. Of course you can't see anything from the bottom of a trench. So we moved out of the way for the wounded and I said to the feller next to me, 'Looks as though they've gone over.'

'Yes, mate,' he says, 'and somebody ain't half stopped a bloomin' packet somewhere, too.'

I put the ammo boxes over my shoulder, thinking, I dunno! If we're going, I wish we'd go and get it over with. But still we stayed there.

This officer came back, then went away. He did this about four times at about twenty-minute intervals. He kept on looking at his watch. The last time he appeared he said, 'Come on, lads. Time we went.'

They had a scaling ladder in this bay: that was a wooden ladder with about four rungs. The officer went first, then the other two chaps, and then me. Of course I had those ruddy ammo boxes and my rifle, so I didn't go over the top with dash as you might say — more of a humping and a scrambling really. No yelling 'Charge' or anything like that.

I kept my eye on the officer just ahead. He turned to

wave us fellers on and then down he went — just as though he was bloody pole-axed. I just kept moving. I wasn't really thinking straight. My job was to keep with the gun-team. 'Don't lose me,' the Number One had said. So I kept on.

And there was blokes laying everywhere. I couldn't see nothing what happened to the left of me because I had my ammunition boxes on that shoulder but where the first waves had been — to my right — there was bodies everywhere and the troops trying to advance had to jump over them. I was running past one fellow — he had a big wound in his leg — and he shouted 'Best of luck to you, mate!' Luck I was certainly going to need, no doubt of that, judging by what was going on. The machine-gun bullets was like a hailstorm. I could see near four hundred yards ahead and to my right, I reckon, and there wasn't a man upright in the middle of No Man's Land. And yet those poor old Newfoundlanders went straight on. You had to admire them. But thinking about it later, I could weep.

Of course the main body of troops was ahead of us. Gun teams are for support and consolidation work. Fellers kept falling down. But the two blokes in front of me kept going down that slope, straight as an arrow. Then the Number Two dropped. We went on. Number One was a big bloke and acted as cover for me behind him. 'Don't lose me,' he'd said. But I lost him in the end. It wasn't long before he went down like a log.

I took a quick look round (quicker than it takes to tell about it). Ahead of me were two Newfoundland blokes — one on the left-hand side was lying well up to the German wire and the other, about twenty-five yards to his right, was spreadeagled over the German wire itself. They were quite dead, there was no doubt. Then there was me. And within a yard of me there was a shell-hole — a nice new shell-hole — it wasn't big, but I couldn't see a better one handy.

I was only young – nineteen. There was no one to give any orders. Boxes of ammunition aren't much good if there's no gun to fire. I couldn't see me charging the whole German army ('cos that's what it sounded like) all on my tod. I couldn't see me winning the battle by my bloody self.

It wasn't a big shell-hole, but I hadn't much choice. I slung the ammunition boxes down and I dived into it. Which was just as well: I must have been sticking out like a sore thumb by then and one of them Jerry machine-gunners decides I'm one too many still standing. Me and the bullets hit the hole pretty near together but I won.

And there I stayed all day. I lay as I fell because I daren't move. I had my legs folded under me and my bloomin' bayonet was on my left-hand side. I was dying to move that bayonet out of the way so I could get my hip down lower. But that Jerry decided he hadn't anything better to do than play his gun across my shell-hole. He knew I wasn't hit. I knew what he was doing. I was a machine-gunner meself, wasn't I? He'd be holding the two handles of his gun, then he'd tap, tap so it played right across the top of the hole; then he'd turn the wheel at the bottom to lower the barrel and then he'd tap, tap the other side to bring it back again. He was hitting the dust just above my head and he smashed the bloomin' boxes. Bits of ammo flew about everywhere. In a queer sort of way I was lying there almost admiring what he was doing, as though it wasn't me he was aiming at. He was a fellow machine-gunner, wasn't he? And he certainly knew his job. But he just couldn't get that trajectory low enough.

I waited all day and it was a long, long day. And it was hot. I was gasping and I was very pleased I'd had no rum because that makes you thirsty. I didn't turn round to look, you may be sure, but I should think I had about four inches of dear old Mother Earth above my head on the Jerry side. But I could see backwards over No Man's Land towards our own lines. Some of the men fallen down were wounded. I saw some of them moving and some turned theirselves over. One man lost his head and stood up and tried to run back. He'd got a terrible wound in his leg and what with the heat and everything I expect he'd gone barmy. He'd got one leg dragging and he tried to get back. He didn't get far. He got peppered. He was dead. You could see the sun glinting on those tin triangles some of them had on the backs of their packs. I lay there and watched it all. I knew there wasn't anything at all I could do until it got dark. And it was summertime. It was a long, long day. I thought to myself, All those training exercises we did round Louvencourt ain't much help here. They tell you the way to go forward, but they don't tell you the way to bloomin' well get back. There was that Sergeant saying, 'Now you're in the second line. Stop and wait for your reinforcements. The reinforcements are coming. They won't be long.' Huh! We hadn't even got as far as the first line. And as to reinforcements − that's a laugh! If those poor devils I can see out there are the reinforcements − well!!! Anyway my problem is how to get back where I came from and all in one piece. I gave a lot of thought to that. And most of the time I was trying to sort it out, that Jerry gunner was nagging away over the top of my hole. Sometimes he'd stop for a bit and turn the gun on someone else; but he'd got right fond of me. Wasted a lot of ammo on me that Jerry did. I didn't see how I was going to get back. None of my training had ever taught me how to do that. But it was obvious I couldn't do anything till it was dark.

I waited and waited and waited while it was getting dusk and I could only see about half-way across No Man's Land. Then it got dark enough for me to try and spread my legs out a bit because they were cramped. Then I heard a 'plop' − it was dark enough for the

Germans to be sending up Very lights and they lit up the whole place just as though the sun was shining. It came down and I calculated I'd got about four seconds to stretch my legs. Another one went up further back but I wasn't bothered about that one. I moved my legs and worked my toes to get the circulation going. 'Plop' – up goes another Very light. When that was down I undid my belt and my shoulder straps, took my gas-bag off and tied a bow on it and put it round my neck. 'Plop' – another Very light – so I froze. I worked out that the Jerry firing those lights was a methodical man; worked as if he was a machine – load, fire, 'plop', sizzle. I wasn't so bothered about him once I'd worked out what he was up to, but I was bothered about this bloke behind me with the machine-gun because he knew I was there somewhere. So I waits for a 'plop' or two and uses the light to look about me. So far as I could see there were only corpses; but some of them were moving when the lights went up and, of course, they got picked off.

I lay in my hole and I worked it all out. I thought, After the next Very light I'll make a bee-line for it. I'd picked out a feller not far away who hadn't moved at all. Next time I made a move. I got behind this bloke and lay on my left-hand side so I could see the way I wanted to go. I thought, I'll have a blow 'ere, I'll get me breath. Then 'plop' and sizzle – some of the lights came down very close to me and they sizzled like Chinese crackers. Off I went again crawling along – not hands and knees, but toes and elbows, hugging the ground. It was slow work and the next light caught me cold, right in the open so I lay stone flat. I remember thinking, Good God, I hope that gunner feller hasn't got his sights right yet. Being a machine-gunner myself I could imagine what he was doing in the trench behind me. So as the second light went down I rolled about six paces away and the dirt flew up from the place where I'd just been. Sounds silly, but I laughed to myself. The next time the Very light goes up he'll look and he'll say, 'The bugger wasn't there at all. I wonder where he's got to?'

And so it went on. The further back I got, the more confident I got. As a matter of fact I got on my hands and knees once or twice to give my toes a rest. Mercifully the Newfoundlanders weren't sending any Very lights up – I was pleased about that. Friend Jerry machine-gunner seemed to have given me up as a bad job and I was very pleased about *that*. There was some stretcher-bearers out because I heard them talking – got to admire them, going out there, chancing their arm to get the wounded in. But I wasn't wounded – yet. I kept going.

Then I found it – a lovely big shell-hole. It was a whopper. They must have dropped a dirty big 'coal-box' (that's what we used to call the big 5.9-inch shells) and it was as big as the bloomin' Eiffel Tower – leastways that's how it looked to me. It was a lovely one, a real topper. I needed a rest by then so in I goes. It was inhabited, as you might say – there was two blokes in there and I judged they were both dead. They looked as if they'd been blown into it, and then tried to crawl out. So I got hold of one feller's legs and pulled him over but he was long since dead. Then, God forgive me because it seemed like robbing a corpse, but I took his water bottle and had a drink. I put it back again when I'd finished. But he didn't need that water and I did. Then I went to have a look at the other bloke; pulled him down, rolled him over and his arm came over slowly and I didn't think he was quite dead. So I did a stupid thing: I patted one side of his face, then the other side and I said to him, 'You all right, mate?' But he didn't answer and he didn't move. So I felt his forehead and it was still warm. Well, I knew where he was if I ever got back, so I gets myself out of that lovely hole and off I goes again.

I'd only gone three or four yards or so when I came to some blinkin' barbed wire. Obviously I couldn't get through it and even if I did, I couldn't get back; but I had to be somewhere near the Newfoundland line by this time. So I listened but I couldn't hear nothing but shells and gun-fire; I couldn't hear any voices. So I shouted, 'It's me. It's me. Where are you? Which is the way in?' I put my hand round my ear and listened but nobody answered. It seemed a pity to get all that way and then not be able to get in the trench. So I screamed my bloomin' head off: 'It's me. Which is the way into the bloody trench?' Somebody shouted back then. 'Hang on. Go to your left. There's a big gap in the wire there.' I crawled to my left and I hadn't gone far before I came to this gap — big enough to take five or six men. So I finally got down into the trench.

And what a bloody fine mess it was, too: blown all ways with shell-fire, and dead laying everywhere. I was getting used to dead bodies by that time. I was only too glad to be out of No Man's Land and away from that flippin' Jerry machine-gunner. So I made my way along as best I could, and I came to a live corporal. He was a stretcher-bearer, that's all I know of him. Never knew his name. He was trying to bandage a bloke who was lying at the bottom of the trench, putting a bandage at the back of his shoulder. And he looked up at me and said, 'Are you the bloke who was shoutin' through the wire just now? Have you been out there all day?' I agreed that was me all right, and I told him about the poor devil in the shell-hole just in front. There was two of 'em, I told the Corporal, but I was damned sure one of them was still alive. So he stood up from the feller he was bandaging and said, 'Show us, then.' So off we went, back through the gap, down into the shell-hole.

The Corporal undid this bloke's tunic and put his ear to his chest. He didn't take any notice of the other man. He was a stretcher-bearer so he'd know it was no use. Then he looked up at me and said, 'Get hold of his webbing.' I didn't understand. 'Bugger his equipment!'

I said. So this Corporal just patiently repeated, 'You get hold of his webbing, like I told you.' Then I understood. So I dug my toes in and grabbed his webbing and then between us we dragged him out and along back into the trench.   We laid him down and the Corporal told me to get his water-bottle. I'll never forget that little scene as long as I live. The Corporal took the bloke's tin hat off and laid his head on it, turned his head to one side and poured some water into one side of his mouth. He coughed and gurgled a bit. All this time the shelling was going on, something terrific. Then the Corporal tried him again with the water and this time the man lifted up his left arm very slowly and tried to get hold of the water-bottle. 'He's all right,' the Corporal said.

'What do I do now?' I asked. He was a corporal, after all, and I felt I could do with some fresh orders. He could see I wasn't one of his lot because of my badges, so he asked me my name and number and told me he thought I'd better buzz off, back to my own unit. This was all in shouts, of course, because of the din. So I buzzed off. Last I see of him he was bending over this bloke we'd got out of the shell-hole. Don't know what happened to the pair of them. I'll never forget it.

I'd got my gas-bag tied round my neck still, but I'd no equipment. Mine was out in No Man's Land somewhere in my first little hole. I knew which way to go because I was facing the eighteen-pounders so I knew I was going back all right. I found a trench to the right and then I came to a place where it looked as though they'd tried to make a bit of an Advanced Dressing Station of it — that's a place where they carried the wounded on stretchers and patched them up a bit. There was lots of equipment and rifles lying about. So I picked up a set of equipment and put it on and also a rifle, but I made sure there was no bloody wire-cutters on the end of this one.

I went along the Newfoundland trenches because I

thought I knew where the Hampshires were: but going up a communication trench I saw some Scottish troops. I wondered where the hell I'd got to. I couldn't find the Hampshires anywhere and I wanted someone to report to.

In the end I found myself out on the road where we used to rendezvous with the limbers so I decided I'd make my way to Englebelmer. All the while the Jerry guns was dropping stuff thick and fast, and roads ain't healthy places when there's shelling. So I got off the road and I passed a great big gun with camouflage on top and they'd built some sandbags up to it. I'd just got past it and for some reason I looked back and I saw a little glimmer of light. So I went back.

When I looked inside the gun emplacement there was a bloke with a canteen of tea in his hand. He had his back to me, so I said, 'Anybody at home?' He turned round. 'Come in,' he says. So I looked at the tea in his hand. 'Good health,' I said.

'Here y'are,' he said. 'Have a drink of tea. You been up front then?'

So I told him I had, I'd been with the Newfoundlanders.

'Gor, blimey!' was his reply. 'What's it like up there?'

I looked at him for a minute. I couldn't tell him. The words wouldn't come. So after a bit I said, 'Smashing place. Hot and cold water laid on. Pretty waitresses rushing about. I wouldn't have missed it for the world.'

You could see he didn't believe me. 'I dunno,' he says, 'no use talking to you is it? Are you hungry? Could you eat a tin of pork and beans?'

'Bloomin' hell, I'm starving,' I said. 'I could eat a bloody boxful, never mind a tin.'

So he opened a tin of pork and beans and told me to finish off the tea and he gave me a fag. 'Where you making for now?' I told him I was trying to find someone to report to, because I was with the Hampshires but they'd booted me out to join the Newfoundlands just for 'the show' and now I didn't know where the Hampshires was: half the poor devils at the front had had it so I thought I might find somebody back at Englebelmer. I thanked him for the tea and that, and said I'd better be buzzing off.

'Cheerio, mate,' he says. 'You got enough fags?' So I said I'd be grateful if he'd got any to spare, so he gave me half a dozen more and away I went.

I'd had a good feed of pork and beans and a bellyful of tea and I'd got some fags. So I was all right. I was quite content. When I got back to Englebelmer I asked for Y Company but nobody seemed to know. I met a corporal and I asked him. He told me that nobody knew where anybody was: him and his lot was waiting for some prisoners. So I said, sarcastic-like, 'Ho, yes. You'll find some prisoners, you will. I *don't* think. You don't want to worry yourself about that.' Then I wandered off and I found an old barn. It was pitch-dark. I thought, This'll do me. I shuffled my feet round to make sure no one was lying there. Cor, I hadn't realized it until that moment, but I was flippin' exhausted. I was absolutely beat. I took my equipment off, undid my belt and lay down, using my haversack as a pillow. I put my tin hat over my face to keep the rats off, crossed my hands, and said a prayer that my father had taught me. It goes like this:

'Here I lie down to sleep,
I give my soul to God to keep
God within, God without
May God surround me all about.

There are four corners to my bed,
There are four angels overhead –
Matthew, Mark, Luke and John
Bless the bed that I lie on.

If any danger touches me
May the Lord awaken me
So let me live, so let me sleep.
I give my soul to God to keep,
for ever, Amen.'

That was my little prayer every night. I said it pretty quickly, then I was gone – unconscious; spark out.

Chapter 4

After The Ball Was Over

'...Many a heart is breaking if we could read them all,
Many the hopes that have vanished – after the ball.'

There were very few soldiers indeed as fortunate as young Private Byrne. He obeyed orders, went on carrying and wiring parties, went out on patrols, and occasionally 'went over the plonk' like everyone else. He certainly did not go looking for trouble in any foolhardy or heroic manner. But it was not necessary to look for trouble in those days because there was plenty of it about and it usually came unbidden. Still he managed to emerge unscathed in 1918 – hence the title of his memoirs. Maybe the quick reflexes of the very young helped; quick thinking later in the war saved him from being shot up by a German aeroplane. His shrewd appraisal of dangerous situations and a well-developed instinct for self-preservation were useful to him. But others had these attributes; a shell-burst or a shower of shrapnel balls can render them quite useless. Perhaps his lucky charm, an unknown saint on a brooch he found in Ypres, exercised a benevolent influence. Whatever it was, he could say thankfully, 'I got through the War, didn't I?'

When Charlie finally crawled in from his shell-hole on the slope above Y Ravine during the night of 1 July 1916, his brief connection with the Newfoundland Regiment was ended. He begins Chapter 4 by relating his return to his own 12 Platoon of Y Company in the 2nd Battalion, the Hampshire Regiment.

I woke up. I could see daylight through the roof and there was a lovely smell of bacon frying somewhere. There was some more blokes in the barn (I thought that I'd a dim feeling about something stumbling over my boots during the night). So I went outside and asked the cook if there was any chance of me getting some tea. 'Where you goin' to put it? In yer 'at?' he says, sarcastic-like (I didn't have no canteen or anything, you see). 'What company do you belong to anyway?' When I told him Y Company, he pointed further down the road and told me where to find them.

That suited me. That was all I wanted to know. That's what I'd been trying to find out all the time. I didn't want no tea or coffee − I just wanted damn 12 Platoon, Y Company. I was happy.

There was our old cook, Bill. When I told him I'd left my canteen in Englebelmer he found me a lid and filled it up with tea − twice. And he gave me some bread and bacon and he let me have some dip for my bread: dip was the lovely greasy bacon fat. Jolly good that was.

Then I walked round to the barn with my rifle on my shoulder and I went inside. I sat down opposite that Corporal − there he was, with all his cronies sitting round him. 'Blimey,' he says to me, 'you still 'ere?' I looked at him for a minute. I'd had enough, I tell you. Then I says, very slow and deliberate, 'I haven't left Louvencourt yet. I stopped in Louvencourt all the while.'

He stared at me. 'What do you mean you stopped in Louvencourt all the while?'

I thought about the day before. I'd had enough.

'You work it out for yerself,' I snaps. Then I swore at him in Hindustani: my old Dad would have been proud of me. I had a good memory and a quick ear and I didn't stutter − not once. I told him what I thought of him and no mistake. I won't bother translating it all: the politest phrase in it was 'shut your mouth'.

He didn't say anything for a long while, just looked at me, and then he said, 'I didn't know you could speak Hindustani.' But he left me alone for a bit after that.

I thought the time had come when we'd finished with being murdered for a bit, but I was wrong. We did nothing all that day but the next night we had carrying party. This Corporal came round. 'You, you, you and you – carrying party.' I was one of the 'yous'. There were so many from each platoon and we got fell in and marched up to the top end of Englebelmer where the dump was. I either had to have a duckboard or a roll of barbed wire and I finished up with the duckboard.

I settled for that, though, because there was blokes worse off than us – they were carrying up gas cylinders. Nasty things they were. This bloomin' ignorant Corporal of ours, he goes right through the standard Army language about how to wear your respirator at the alert. As though we didn't know by this time! He loved the sound of his own voice, that Corporal did. Anyway off we go with our respirators on. We were carrying up just to the east of a little village on the left of Beaumont-Hamel – Auchonvillers I think it might have been. It was a long journey up there and it was no blinkin' picnic that night. We had a lot of blokes wounded. I kept thinking about those gas cylinders. I didn't like it and I was very glad when we dumped our loads and started back again. Then my heart sank right down into my boots, right to the bottom of them! The orders were that we had to do another journey. That was absolutely bloomin' punishment. But we did it.

I was on again the next night, too, but they treated us lightly this time. It wasn't any funnier than the night before, but at least we only had to do one journey – they'd come to the conclusion that two journeys in one night was too much for us. Bloomin' 'eck, we must have been fit in those days!

Anyway, while I was waiting around at the dump I

heard one of the old soldiers talking to another one. We had to have our respirators at the alert again, because gas cylinders were going up (I didn't have one of them, I'm pleased to say). But I heard this old soldier say to his mate, 'My bloody respirator's no good. We've been wearing them at the alert all the while and they're bone dry. Something wrong 'ere.'

So I pricked my ears up. When I got back in the billet I pulled my gas-bag out and had a proper look at it and he was right, it was bone-dry. They were supposed to be soaked with chemicals and this looked like an ordinary piece of rag. So I sat and I did a lot of thinking about that, and then I remembered Lieutenant Morley and the listening patrol. 'Come and see me,' he'd said.

That was all very well, but where was he? I hadn't seen him since and I'd no idea where to look. But the next time I had a few hours spare I wandered off to another village nearby called Mailly-Maillet to try my luck. And my luck was in.

First bloke I saw going up the street was very smart — boots all clean, puttees all done right — so I knew he must be an officer's servant. So I asked him about Lieutenant Morley, and he said the Lieutenant was in the old chateau: the top was all off but the officers' mess was down below.

When I got there, I tapped on his door and he told me to come in. He looked up. 'Hullo, Byrne,' he said. 'How are you getting on?' 'All right, Sir,' I said, 'I went over the other day but I got back all right.'

'We had it pretty rough, too,' he says. 'I see you've still got that speech impediment of yours. Nerves, that's what that is, nerves.'

I was a bit put out. 'I don't feel bloody nervous, Sir.'

'No, I don't mean wind-up. Different kind of nerves. I know a doctor back in Canada who could help you with that. But what can I do for you? If it's money you want to borrow,' and he laughed, 'I can't help you there.'

'No,' I said, 'I don't want any money, thank you.'

'Do you know where we're bound for when we leave here?' he said.

'No, Sir.'

(Well, I did have a pretty good idea because I'd heard fellers talking. But it gave me the lead I wanted.)

'Going to Ypres,' said the Lieutenant.

'Notorious place for gas? Right, Sir?'

'Right you are, Byrne. The old Canadians got a right bashing round there earlier in the war. But I shan't be going. I'm going to the Base for a course. I'm going to Etaples.' (We used to call it Eel-taps, but of course he pronounced it properly).

Things were going really well for me. 'You won't need a respirator down Eel-taps, will you, Sir?' I says. 'So can I have yours?' I knew his would be better than mine.

'Certainly you can have mine,' he says, a bit puzzled. 'But what's the matter with yours?'

So I showed him mine and he agreed it was certainly u/s and I could have his, because he could get another one down at the Base. So I went off well satisfied. I didn't say nothing to nobody when I got back. No use. They'd all moan if something was wrong, plenty would make the bullets but nobody would shoot 'em. I wasn't going to. If I'd complained to the Sergeant, he'd likely give me seven days. I dunno. He might've listened, I suppose. But I didn't think so.

Sure enough a few days later we marched off, got on a train and went up to Ypres. We detrained at Poperinghe and we marched up to a place called either Vlamertinghe or Elverdinghe, I forget which. There was four places I used to think of as the 'inges – Poperinghe, Vlamertinghe, Elverdinghe and Boesinghe and we were billeted in the second one. We had a nice time there. There were still some civilians living there and I was very interested to see some of these old Belgian ladies sitting outside their houses making lace. They had a kind of round table on their knees and a cushion thing with long bobbins with bits of white cotton on them: and they used to throw one bobbin over the other, and over again and then stick a pin in – this cushion thing was full of pins. There was all these bobbins flying about here and there so fast. It was really fascinating. I wandered around this village free as a bird. It was a nice change walking about on top of the land instead of being in the bloody trenches all the while.

During my wanderings I found the transport lines and I got friendly with the blokes there. The Sergeant was called Smith: he was a Londoner, belonged to the Essex Regiment – they was in 88 Brigade, 29th Div., same as us.

I used to spend a lot of my time round the transport lines. I was quite happy with the mules. When the Sergeant blew the whistle for watering-time I'd go along and see if any were left behind. To save a second journey I'd ask the old Sergeant if I could take one down. 'Yes, Ginge,' he'd say. 'Make yourself useful if you want to. Take down a couple. Get on.' They had no bits or stirrups or saddles or anything, because you don't want to believe all you hear about mules. They're docile creatures really. I used to spend more of my spare time down the transport lines than I did anywhere else. They was company. I liked mules.

One day, about half past one, the old Corporal come up to me and said, 'I've got a nice job for you.' Blimey, I thought, *nice* job! He must have had a change of heart! He told me he wanted to see me the next morning in clean fatigue dress, no equipment, just my gas-mask.

So next morning after breakfast (fried bacon – jolly good – but I couldn't get any dip for me bread) off I goes. We went down the main road towards Ypres and there was a big field with some latrines in. It was quite a posh place really. It had tall canvases about eight or ten foot high and about twenty-five feet long with a little bit just to cover round the side — I take it that was so the civilian people wouldn't see blokes using the buckets. There was long planks with buckets under: two sorts of buckets — one to piddle in and one for your Number Two. I soon cottoned on to what the bloomin' nice job was! The drier stuff had to be chucked in an incinerator.

The Corporal took me over to the incinerator and said, 'You'll have a fatigue party coming up soon.' (I was going to be in charge of somebody apparently!) Anyway, he soon buzzed off, he didn't stop long — there was a stink and a lot of flies.

So while I was waiting I had a good butcher's hook round. I got a lot of twigs and stuff and made a blazing fire for the incinerator. Then I just waited for further orders.

After a while up come a Pioneer Corporal with a gang of big tall blokes with a sort of blue uniform made of some coarse stuff and they had brass bands on their left arms with numbers on. He left eight of them with me and marched the rest further up the road.

Well, they were Chinese Labour Corps blokes! I didn't know what they had to do. Can you imagine me talking to a lot of bloody Chinamen? But one of them had obviously been there before, he seemed to know his bill all right. He jabbered away at me in Chinese, so I just nodded me head. He started off carrying the buckets to the incinerator: he was a bloody good bloke, but the others were just skivers. They were only carrying one bucket at a time: so I gets this bloke and I picked up one bucket, and stood with one shoulder low down, then I picked up another and stood level — to show him it was better to be balanced, see. He seemed to be an intelligent bloke. He got it. I got the job done. So I give him a couple of fags when it was finished.

When I got back to the billet that night I got an idea. I knew I'd have to go back the next day. I didn't need any telling. Nobody else would do it. So I got my razor out and cut a stripe off an old overcoat that was lying about with some old rags and stuff. I'd make my Chink a lance-corporal – temporary, acting, unpaid. So when the Pioneer Corporal marched 'em up the next day I looked along the line and picked him out. People say they all look alike, like mules, but they don't. He had a perpetual smile on his face – lovely set of teeth he had. 'Can I have that one?' I said to the Corporal.

'Makes no bloody difference to me which ones you 'ave,' he said, 'so long as you got eight.' So off he goes with the squad.

I pinned the stripe on this Chinaman's arm and I give him a bit of stick. 'There,' I said, explaining the best way I could, 'you be the bloody gaffer then.' And, by Christ, he didn't half make the others work, worked like crackers they did. Got the job done in three-quarters of the time! When we'd finished, we all sat round waiting for the Pioneer Corporal to come back. They were chatting and jabbering away quite happy and showing me the numbers on the brass bands round their arms.

Next day the same. All I had to do was keep the incinerator fire going. I was happy. So when the Pioneer blokes came to collect them, I said to him, 'See you in the morning.'

'If you're here, you will,' he answered. 'But they don't usually stop here more than two or three days. You'll find you'll be buzzing off up the line soon.'

And he was quite right. I didn't see the Chinks again, because we marched up to Ypres that very night.

We went across the railway line at Ypres; there was a big gasometer on the left and the Cloth Hall and we'd turn right and go to the Ypres Cellars. They were underneath a convent, but that had gone though the cellars were still there. The Menin Gate and the Ramparts were more or less straight ahead. We stopped in there three days. The second night me and another feller thought we'd like a look in the Cathedral. It was all ruined. We were a bit silly, foolhardy you might say, but everything was fairly quiet — for Ypres that is — and we were nosey, so we went to have a look. What a mess! We climbed around in the rubble. There were a lot of papers scattered about and then I saw something glinting. I stooped and picked it up. It was a brooch, ever so pretty. It was about the size of the old half-crowns with a pin on the back and it had the figure of a woman on it — like Joan of Arc or somebody like that — and silver leaves round it. I pinned it inside my tunic and I wore it right through the War. I kept it right up to the time when I come to live in the house I'm in now. I always meant to take it back after the War if ever I got the opportunity to go to Ypres. After all if that figure was some saint or other, it had done me proud. I got through the War, didn't I? Which was more than a lot did. I thought it really ought to go back to the Cathedral, because it didn't belong to me by rights. I did get the chance to go back to Ypres, but I didn't take the brooch back.

Chapter 5

Gas!

'Gas! Gas! Quick, boys! – An ecstasy of fumbling,
Fitting the clumsy helmets just in time;
But someone still was yelling out and stumbling
And flound'ring like a man in fire or lime...
Dim through the misty panes and thick green light,
As under a green sea, I saw him drowning.'

('Dulce et Decorum est' by Wilfred Owen)

So, in the third week of July 1916, the 25th Division relieved the 29th. Most battalions had received large drafts of men to replace the casualties of the first day of the Somme, but the Worcesters and the Hampshires had been in reserve and had not suffered as heavily: in 12 Platoon, Y Company of the 2nd Hampshires it was, more or less, 'as you were'.

A number of things in the life of young Private Byrne were going to change. He emerged from the excitement around Ypres and transferred to the Machine Gun Corps. That pleased him. He stayed with the Division. He was attached to 88 Brigade and soldiered right to the end with them.

The 29th Division were in the Ypres sector for about two months. During that time Private Byrne survived a gas attack which cost the lives of about three hundred of his comrades. He may or may not be correct in the rather bitter conclusions he draws from this incident. (The official reports of this attack are given in Appendix I.)

We went up the line from Ypres, the 2nd Hampshires did. The line there wasn't continuous trenches like it was on the Somme: Somme country was chalk and you could make good trenches there – Jerry did, anyhow. Ours weren't as good; I suppose the higher-ups didn't want us to make ourselves too comfortable. But up in the Salient it was clay and it was always wet; dig a couple of feet down and all you'd get would be a hole full of water. So we made breastworks of sandbags instead of trenches. They ran along for about six feet, then there was a space of about six feet, then some more sandbags and so on. There was a bit of a trench behind the breastwork but it was very shallow. That was the front line. Then behind that was the second line – same sort of thing but the breastworks there covering the gap in front, if you get my meaning. You might as well be in the second line as in the front line really: didn't make a lot of odds in the Salient because gas was the big thing there and gas sort of hugs the ground, and if it gets in the bottom of deep trenches it takes a while to disperse.

We went in about 4th or 5th of August and it was nice and quiet. Seems funny to think of the Salient being quiet, but at that time it was; nice change from Beaumont-Hamel. We were allowed to take our shirts off and chat 'em out (that's getting the lice out of them, or at least trying to: lice was the only real born survivors in war). Jerry was only holding the line with gas and snipers; you had to be careful about them, of course, but it was pretty peaceful. One day I saw an old sergeant's tunic lying around (very untidy battlefields are, there's always rusty tins and bits of equipment and stuff from men who've died previous: if there hadn't been time or opportunity to clean up you'd often get bits of the men as well!) so I took a razor and cut the stripes off this tunic because I was entitled, on 10th August 1916, to put a two-year badge up; so I sewed my badge on.

This bloody Corporal comes along and stares at my

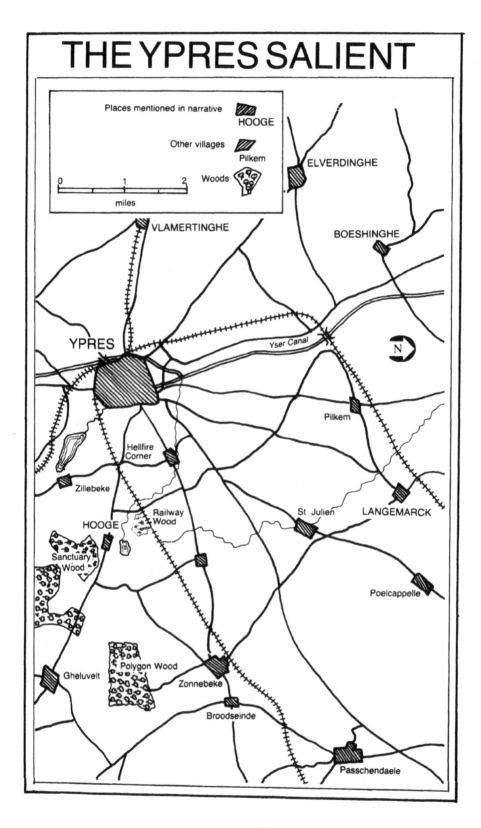

THE YPRES SALIENT

Places mentioned in narrative — HOOGE

Other villages — Pilkem

Woods

0   1   2
miles

ELVERDINGHE

BOESHINGHE

VLAMERTINGHE

YPRES

Yser Canal

N

Pilkem

Hellfire Corner

Zillebeke

Railway Wood

HOOGE

St Julien

LANGEMARCK

Sanctuary Wood

Poelcappelle

Polygon Wood

Gheluvelt

Zonnebeke

Broodseinde

Passchendaele

Charlie's father, Daniel Byrne, also a private in the Hampshire Regiment, 'a smart man he was, with a ginger moustache'. He had served in the Burma and South African Wars, and died in 1917, while Charlie was in France.

Charlie's oldest brother, Jim, who was killed with the Hampshires at Gallipoli on 4 June 1915. It was Jim who told the 2nd Hampshires' CO that Charlie was not nineteen when he enlisted, thus probably saving his youngest brother from the fate that he himself suffered.

Transport lighters at Gallipoli, 1915, with mules being offloaded. 'The Hampshires got knocked about something cruel round Gully Ravine.'

Charlie Byrne in uniform, just after he had joined up in 1914.

A Canadian machine-gun team on the Somme, 1916; the weapon is a Vickers .303, the standard heavy machine-gun in service throughout the British, Dominion and Empire forces in the Great War (and, indeed, in the Second World War).

A German photograph of the village of Beaumont-Hamel in 1916, where the Newfoundland Regiment, to which Charlie was attached on 1 July, came to grief. It was finally taken in November 1916; six months later one military observer wrote: 'There is nothing to be seen of Beaumont-Hamel. . . . The whole ground is overlapping craters . . . '.

A British patrol in No Man's Land in front of Beaumont-Hamel, 1 July 1916.

A British 15-inch howitzer being readied for action on the outskirts of Englebelmer, a few miles south-west of Beaumont-Hamel, and a village Charlie came to know well. The British artillery barrage in preparation for 1 July was then the greatest ever fired — but it still failed in its object.

Vlamertinghe, a town some two miles due west of Ypres. 'We had a nice time there', said Charlie. 'There were still some civilians living there . . . [and] it was a nice change walking about on top of the land instead of being in the bloody trenches.'

The ruins of the Cloth Hall at Ypres, a photograph taken in 1916, at about the time Charlie was there. By the war's end not even these ruins were standing.

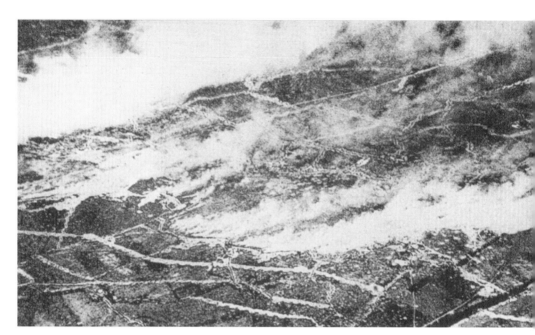

An aerial photograph of a gas attack in progress, showing clearly how such attacks relied upon a steady prevailing wind. Changes in wind direction could be crucial, as Charlie was well aware: '. . . if there's a slight gust blowing this way, keep your bloomin' ears open for the gas. It sort of hisses,' he warned a comrade.

A Vickers-gun team wearing one of the early, not always very effective, types of gas-mask. Charlie's life was saved during a gas attack near Ypres in August 1916 because he had begged a serviceable respirator from a Canadian officer. His mates were not so lucky.

A Mark IV tank on the move at the Graincourt side of Flesquières Ridge, 1917; on the left is a German field-gun. 'Bloody silly using tanks at Ypres; they just got bogged down in all that mud – pathetic really', was Charlie's comment.

A Canadian machine-gun team at Passchendaele, 14 November 1917, just eight days after Canadian troops had finally taken the village – or what remained of it. The battle had started on 31 July, and cost the British more than 300,000 casualties; mud, as much as the Germans, was the enemy for the attacking troops.

The Newfoundland Memorial Park at Beaumont-Hamel on the Somme, 1 July 1978, the sixtieth anniversary of the start of the battle. Charlie Byrne, then aged eighty-one, lays a wreath in memory of his comrades of the Royal Newfoundland Regiment, which took savage casualties during its attack on 1 July 1916. 'Think of that! Me, a plain bloody private, laid them wreaths,' he said afterwards in astonished pride.

arm. 'What's that?' he says. 'Who told you to put that badge up?' I said, 'I'm entitled to two years come 10th August.' 'Take it off. Take it off. Come along o' me.' And off he fusses down the communication trench to the second line and I'm follerin'.

Of course there's no guard-room nor nothing, just a scrape-out with an army blanket hung in front and a piece of corrugated iron over the top. Inside there was an officer down on his hunkers writing something on a bit of board: it wasn't what you'd call roomy and when you 'ad to go in front of the officer you 'ad to get down like the pictures you used to see of bloody Gandhi! I felt like booting that Corporal up the backside while he was bending down telling the officer all about it because he was in a lovely bloomin' position for me to give him a real right fourpenny one. But he stood up before I give way to the temptation, and I was glad afterwards that I didn't. The officer said, 'You're not allowed to put a two-year badge on your arm until it comes out in Battalion Orders. Take it off.' So I said, 'Very good, Sir.' I couldn't stand up and salute him or I'd of hit the top of me bloomin' head on the tin roof. When I stood up outside, he says, 'Corporal, give him some jankers.' Jankers! Cor blimey, what do you do with a pair like that, I ask you? Jankers — out *there* — ruddy stupid. But they did. They stuck me out on bloody wiring out the front.

But even so that queer luck of mine was in again because if I hadn't been out wiring I might not have been quite so nippy. It was on the night of the 9th or early morning of the 10th of August — I might be a day out either way. There was a lot of us fellers on this wiring party, but I suppose I wouldn't have been there if I hadn't been doing jankers. After a bit I heard this unfamiliar noise. Like a steam engine it was.

I thought to myself, What the bloody hell's that? Not bloomin' MG fire nor artillery. Bloody hell! It's bloody gas! Near me was one of those empty eighteen-pounder shells strung on a bit of wood with a stick lying beside it – a gas gong. So I give this thing a great bash and down into the trench I dives with all the wiring party coming in behind me. I puts Lieutenant Morley's respirator on, tucked it inside my collar, did my top button up. I could feel the blood vessels at the side of my neck pump away. And there I stood.

Didn't take me long to do all that and all the while you could hear the warning taken up all along the line – gas gongs going everywhere and I was the first one who had given the signal. You could hear them all behind the line where the artillery blokes was banging these gongs. It was a right palaver for a bit. God knows how the poor fellows going along the roads with the rations was getting on with the mules, because they got no bloomin' gas-masks for mules. I kept thinking about those poor mules.

But we got gassed well and truly; they made a proper bloomin' job of it with phosgene and chlorine. I reckon I had my gas-bag on for well over an hour. I stood up on the fire-step with my arms across my chest, because my training was keep upwards from gas, don't get down low and you kept your arms up like that to stop it creeping up your clothes. I'd been well-trained, and I reckoned if I kept a cool head, kept my presence of mind, I'd be all right. But it wasn't easy. While I stood there I could feel fellers' arms pulling at my legs, trying to drag themselves up off the floor. I could hear them grunting and making funny kinds of noises. There was nothing I could do to help them.

After a long time I heard a voice from about two bays up shouting, 'Get your respirators off. Everything's all clear now. Get your respirators off, everybody.' I don't know whether there was anybody there that could hear him or not. I kept mine on. Then this sergeant come past me. 'Oi, you! All right now,' he said and tapped me on the arm. So I could see he hadn't got his on, so I took mine off and got down in the trench alongside him. I could see his buttons were the same colour as my brass bell up on the mantelpiece at home, but mine were all green and brown. They're going to take some polishing up, I thought.

'Are you all right?' he asked, looking at me a bit queer.

'Yes, I'm all right. These poor buggers ain't, though, are they?'

The poor devils were laying about there with sort of soap-suds coming out of their mouths and the soap-suds kept on coming out. Lot of them died with their left leg and their left arm up. It was a terrible sight. To get along the trench I had to step over them and they looked at you. I don't know if they were quite dead or had died with their eyes open. I don't know whether their eyes registered, whether they could see or whether they were like that permanently. But they looked up at you. Then I came to this Corporal and I stepped over him. I don't know whether he recognized me or not, but I thought to myself, You won't say to me again 'Are you bloody well still 'ere?' Will you? But I bloody well am. But when he looked up at me with all the soap-suds coming out of his mouth I didn't feel nothing against him. Truly I just felt bloody sorry. I should think there was a lot of people with unserviceable gas-masks there. When a bloke is choking to death he tears his mask off, so they hadn't got them on but they'd certainly have put them on when they heard the gas gongs. We was all well trained. I never remember anybody testing them to see they were serviceable. It must have been somebody's bleedin' job to see they were tested, musn't it? Anyway, those that were left came out of the trench — it wasn't many. I don't remember anybody except a Corporal Butchers — he was gassed; he was still able to stand up but he was short of breath and I don't think he lasted out.

The next day we were relieved — the Bedfordshires I think it was, but I'm not sure now. We left all our dead there, and one of their fellers coming in said to me, 'You've had a bloody rough time here, haven't you?'

'Yes,' I said. 'But here's a tip. You keep your eye on that.'

'That' was a little cross with two bits of cotton hanging down with two bits of wadding tied on – hanging loose.

'Keep your eye on that. You watch which way they're blowing. If they're blowing away from you, you're all right: but if there's a slight gust blowing this way, keep your bloomin' ears open for the gas. It sort of hisses.'

He thanked me for that. But that little life-saver wasn't an Army issue, thought up by some clever bloke at the Base. It was a thing an ordinary common private soldier had thought of and made. It was very simple.

'By the way,' I said to this bloke, 'I 'ope you've 'ad your gas-mask tested!' And off I went. I knew my road back all right. On the way back I see the poor old mules, some laying about and some with their muzzles touching the ground – got a whiff, see. Poor devils.

I got back to Ypres and there's the same old field-cooker outside the convent cellars with old Bailey, the cook. He was doing his extra twenty-one years was old Bailey. I don't know whether he was joking or not, but when he sees me he says, 'Have some bully stew, Charlie. Plenty of bloody stew to go round tonight.'

'You're bloomin' tellin' me!' I said. So I had a good feed of stew, pulled the blanket back and went down into the cellars. It was a massive place: you could sleep twenty blokes each way and twenty sideways. I couldn't see in the dark so I just fumbled my feet about to see there was a space, lay down and I was gone.

Next thing I knew, somebody had pulled the blanket back beside the door and a voice said, 'Anybody there?' Somebody answered and there were about five voices after that. When I said 'Yes, I'm here,' the voice said, 'Is that you, Byrne?' I could just see the shape against the daylight outside – riding breeches and the shape of the tunic, and together with the voice I recognized Lieutenant Layton. He called me outside. 'What happened, Byrne? Didn't they get their gas-masks on in time?'

I'd begun to realize just how empty those cellars were compared to what they had been.

'Oh! Yes,' I says, 'they got 'em on all right but they was no bloody good.'

He didn't answer me. He just went away and left me there. I thought, Now what have I done wrong? Perhaps he was offended at the language I'd used. I used to put in a lot of little swear words like that, because of this bad impediment in my speech: I sort of felt it helped me to get things out better. No one in the cellar said anything when I went back in so I had a bit of a doze.

It would be about half an hour or so later when a bloke poked his head through the blanket and called my name and told me I was wanted in the Orderly Room. So I went with him; no equipment nor nothing and I wasn't too tidy; and we picked our way along through the rubble in the back streets. The Orderly Room was in a cellar, of course, with a gas-blanket over the door and there was a big table with an officer sitting behind it.

'You a machine-gunner?' he asked me.

'Yessir.'

'Would you be interested in going in the Machine Gun Corps?'

I said I'd love to.

'Right!' said the officer. 'Unfortunately you'll be back tonight in the line where you've just come from, but you won't be in the front line. You'll be in the second line.'

Thank you very much! I thought to meself.

But out loud I said, 'Very good. I shan't need a guide. I know my way back all right. So I consider myself transferred to the Machine Gun Corps from now on? When do I go back in the line? After stand-to?'

'Yes,' he mumbled. 'Safest time.'

So I saluted and went out.

So I'm in the Machine Gun Corps and very pleased about it, too. But I was right, you know. The gas-masks were no good. Blokes had them on and they died in them. If I hadn't had this bump of — what do they call it? — self-preservation, and got me an officer's gas-bag, I'd have been a goner, too.

Chapter 6

Here and There in 1917 with the Machine Gun Corps

'There's a long, long trail a-winding
Into the land of my dreams
Where the nightingales are singing
And a white moon beams.
There's a long, long night of waiting,
Until my dreams all come true....'

During the autumn of 1916 Charlie was in 88 Brigade's Machine-gun Company. That autumn the 29th Division was back on the Somme, though quite a distance away from Beaumont-Hamel this time. Roughly speaking, the scene of their activities was between the road which runs from Flers to Ligny Thilloy on the left and Sailly-Saillisel on the right. The weather at the end of September and the beginning of October was deplorable. The bleak east wind brought incessant downpours of cold rain. The sticky, chalky mud of the Somme became as notorious as the bogs round Ypres.

On 12 October 88 Brigade was detached from the 29th Division and sent to the 12th Division to help with an attack at Gueudecourt: this was part of one of the later battles that make up the Somme series.

The rest of 1916 was passed in the Cavillon area; 88 Brigade being now back with the 29th Division at Molliens-Vidame.

The early months of 1917 were bitterly cold and frosty. The 29th was relieved in March by the Guards Division and, after a short period of rest, trudged up to Arras to take part in the later stages of the First Battle of the

Scarpe in April and in the early operations in the Second Battle of the Scarpe.

One of the focal points of 88 Brigade's responsibilities was the village of Monchy-le-Preux. It is five miles south-east by east of the railway station at Arras on the summit of a conical hill and commands extensive views of the surrounding countryside. Germans and British fought bitterly for its possession.

Mr Byrne recalls Monchy clearly enough, but as he himself put it: 'I'm a bit lost after Monchy.' His memories of Flers and Combles almost certainly belong with 88 Brigade's sojourn on the Somme in early 1917, because when his Division was withdrawn from the Arras battles at the beginning of June there was a period of rest and training, and then it was sent up to Flanders to take part in the Third Battle of Ypres.

This is popularly known to history as 'Passchendaele' after the village on the summit of one of the encircling hills that formed the infamous Salient. Although it was officially one battle, like the Somme it was really a campaign which consisted of a number of engagements – Pilckem Ridge, Langemarck, Menin Road Ridge, Polygon Wood, Broodseinde, Poelcappelle and Passchendaele itself.

The precise reasons why the campaign was undertaken and the arguments as to whether it should have been undertaken at all are outside the scope of this story. Private Byrne knew nothing of such matters. Sufficient for him that he was there. What he did know about in great detail were the slimy canals, sloughs, bogs, slippery duckboards, incessant shelling, mists and fogs, isolated outposts, corpses and gas and dreadful smells that formed the back-drop of his existence. He took these things so much for granted that he scarcely mentions them.

So I'm in the Machine Gun Corps. I was fully qualified. I could do anything with a machine-gun. I liked it better in the Machine Gun Corps because they were a cosmopolitan sort of crowd; came from all different regiments. There was Scotsmen, Irishmen, Jews – you name it and there they was, all the blinking breeds and religions; so everybody started off on a par. I was as happy as a sandboy in 88 Brigade Machine Guns.

We left Ypres and went down Arras way and I knew we were going to entrain and I had an idea. I didn't like those trains. I knew the transport had lost a lot of mules and a lot of blokes. So I went down the transport lines and I see this sergeant. I knew they had a lot of mules coming up from the depot – remounts they called them. But I knew they were short of drivers. So I went to see the old sergeant there. Smith his name was. He was a Jew-boy, kept a stall down in Walworth in London in peacetime. Proper lad he was. I asked him if he wanted a hand with some of the donkeys.

'If you want to,' he says. 'There's plenty here. But can you handle mules?'

'I can handle a bloomin' rhinoceros if you want, never mind a mule.'

'There's some right Barbary wallahs there,' he warned me. (In Army Hindustani a Barbary Wallah is a wicked fellow; a real bad boy).

'If you can handle them I'll see if I can get you made a driver when we get to Arras.'

'They'll be all right with me,' I promised him.

So I got a ride on a donkey all the way to Arras. I loved it. We went in fours – two in front and two behind but I wasn't in front because they'd got a proper driver in front. Of course the back ones would follow the front ones anyway, but you had to have a driver on them as well. We went along the road and camped out at night. We used to extend the limbers out about thirty yards apart, put a rope along, tie the mules up and give them their water and their nose-bags; then we'd put up a bell-tent to sleep in. We'd knock it down again the next morning, pack it all up, then away we'd go again through

73

the villages. It took about four days. I did enjoy it. We ended up on Arras racecourse. Then I got sent to my unit and I didn't hear any more about being a driver. I expect the Sergeant forgot.

From Arras we had to go into a place called Monchy-le-Preux. You went through Arras, down the road towards Bapaume, and down to a crossroads by a chalk pit. There was a nasty bit of road there for about a kilometre. It had trees each side and Jerry had a bloomin' set of guns trained on there. It was a battery of three and he used to drop three shells here, three there and three in the middle. Then he'd do it again. He plastered that bit of road night and day. It was littered with bloomin' broken-down limbers and dead mules and dead blokes. You didn't linger there looking at the view, I can tell you.

But I did stop there for a while one day. We was coming back from Monchy and we'd just got past the crossroads, past this wicked piece of road and I saw this team of four. Three of them were dead, but there was this poor creature standing in the wheel (she was a wheel-mule) with her head down low. So I said to my mate, 'I can't leave her there, poor devil. And I can't bring meself to putting a bullet through her either.' So I went over to cut her loose. 'Come on,' said my mate, 'let it alone, will yer.' He wanted to get on. Nobody liked mucking about on that piece of road. But I didn't listen. I got her out and took her down the transport lines and she was all right. I gave her a name and all: I used to call her Munchy. We went right through the war together. People say mules is like Chinamen − you can't tell one from another − but you can, you know, when you know them that is. She was a nice little mule, my Munchy. The transport blokes said she was quite old: one of them reckoned she'd been through the South African War. I used to go and see her in the transport lines. I don't know what happened to her after the war.

Very hard-worked those animals were; still, so were we for that matter.

Not that there was a great deal happening up the front at that time apart from the usual nastinesses. But there was always carrying parties and ration parties and wiring parties. We were always humping something from here to there. The mules could only get so far towards the front line because of the mud; then a man'd take over and hump it on his back. But it was one of the few things I'd ever volunteer for – rations, you understand, and rations were very important in the front line.

So if anybody said, 'Anybody know where the transport lines are?' I used to pop up straightway and say, 'Yes, I do.' The old Sergeant used to say, 'All right. But Christ 'elp you if you lose yourself.' It was important not to lose yourself. If you can imagine, it was dark and the going was bad – really bad if you couldn't get the mules any further – and there were no signposts or nothing and nobody to ask. If the bloke in front lost 'isself then the whole party would be standing there under bloomin' shell-fire not knowing what to do nor where to go. You can't ask anybody so you've got to have it all in your noddle.

Not to brag, but I had a gift for it and I trained myself too. I used to look back over my shoulder going out to see what the countryside would look like when I was going back and I noticed everything I could. It was always in the dark so you had to have sharp eyes for things on the sky-line like stumps of trees or dead mules and horses or a bit of wire sticking up queer – things like that. That's one thing I will say, I never lost my way once. I had one or two near-misses, mind, but I always got there with the rations in the finish.

Only other thing I remember about Monchy was one bit of excitement where the infantry was supposed to break through and then the cavalry was going to take over – Strathcona's Horse I think it was. The cavalry!

You might as well have kept them in England for all the good they were. Cavalrymen used to fight dismounted sometimes and very good they were, but galloping horses across No Man's Land with all them shell-holes? Ridiculous! The only reason I remember this particular bit of nonsense was because when we were marching back from Monchy we went past Arras racecourse and they'd got the horses ready there. It was a bitter cold winter and the horses had been clipped to look smart and they were used to living in nice warm stables. For the break-through they'd been picketed out ready for the off and a lot of them froze to death. Poor animals! Bloody heart-breaking it was!

I'm a bit lost after Monchy. I remember going to the station at Arras: it was down flat of course; most of Arras was flat − lot of shelling there and the Germans were just on the edge of it at one point. Under Arras there was a honeycomb of tunnels: they had footpaths with the names of the streets up and all underneath Arras. You could go underground from Arras practically up to the chalk pits but of course you couldn't take mules down there.

Where did we go from there? I think we went south to a place called Combles. Going into the line at Combles there was a certain part of the way going in over a bit of a hill that was open to artillery fire, and they put netting up. That wouldn't stop the shells naturally, but they couldn't see you go through − camouflage like. Just before you got there, there was an old house that had been partly knocked down but you could see into the bedroom and there was a bedstead there, all knocked about, and hung on it was a pair of women's knickers and a skirt and a couple of blouses. Funny to think it had all stayed there all through the shelling! But we used to call that Pawn Shop Corner.

There was a lot of Corners in France and Belgium. There was Windy Corner − no need to explain that: they used to say even the Guards got 'wind-up' round there. Somewhere else there was Dead Cow Corner, where there was an old white cow dead; well, there was just the skin of it left really. But the one that makes me laugh to remember was a corner in Ypres. Lot of Corners there – Sniper's Corner, Hell Fire Corner. But when we used to march up to Ypres there was a big gasometer on the left-hand side just as you go over the railway and it was all cockeyed. Jerry used to send over these bloomin' great 'coal boxes' ranging on the Cathedral and the Cloth Hall, trying to flatten 'em. Bloody well succeeded too. Anyway, one of these must have landed wrong, it must have skidded along the road and not gone off. I don't know whether it was a dud or not – bloomin' great big shell with a big point on it, would fill up an ordinary living-room, huge great thing. Somebody coming out of the line had rolled it to the side of the road out of the way and put some wire-netting over it to stop any fool messing about with it. Some wag, some bloody comedian, had chalked on the side of it 'A bird in a gilded cage' after the music-hall song. So it was always Gilded Cage Corner. I expect the rain washed the chalk off eventually. There was plenty of rain round Ypres.

But I'm going off my story. After Arras we went down the Somme again – Flers and Combles way. At Flers you could get best part of the way towards the line under cover by a wood, but after that you were in the open. But Jerry didn't seem to bother opening up on you if there was only four or five fellers; didn't waste his ammo on anything less than a platoon. Anyway, we had to take up two duckboards, two bundles of sandbags, two petrol cans of water and two boxes of ammunition – there was five of us and two mules. The donkeys would have the load as far as they could go, then the fifth feller would take them back and the other four would go plodding on.

Well, I knew before we started I'd get those duckboards. I knew it. We had to wait around a bit before we started (you did a lot of waiting around in the Army) and I had an idea. Remember me telling you about those bits of wadding on cotton that told you which way the wind was blowing in case of gas at Ypres? Well, my idea wasn't Government Issue either, but it worked. It was like this – lying around the transport depot was some huge tarpaulin sheets with big long ropes on that they used to cover up the hay and fodder for the animals. So, when no one was looking, I took my jack-knife and cut off two of these ropes and rolled them up in my haversack. About quarter of an hour later we made our way through Happy Valley (don't let the name cheer you up at all – it was nothing but a bloomin' muddy place) and got to the edge of this wood I was telling you about. There the mules were sent back. Sure enough, I got the duckboards. I knew I would. The feller with the sandbags had the best carry. Off the others went, but I fastened my ropes round the middle of each duckboard, one on each side of me, then I put the ropes across my shoulders and I'd got my hands free to steady the duckboards. Tell you what it was like – remember the way they carried water and milk in buckets in the old days? A yoke I think they called it – it was as simple as that.

The others were ahead of me by this time, skirting round the shell-holes and, of course, they had to put their loads down to rest their arms now and again, but I just kept plodding on and gradually caught them up. I passed them in the end and, as I went by, I lifted my arms out straight and flapped them like a bird. They laughed; thought it was a good idea. They asked me where I got the rope from but I wasn't telling them that or I'd have got into trouble for sabotaging Army property, so I told them I'd found it lying about. So we goes past Dead Cow Corner, up the communication trench, up John Bull trench, dumps the loads and off we saunters back.

It would have been cheap and easy for the Government

to issue every soldier with about six or eight foot of rope — I don't mean tow-rope, something like sash-cord would have done. Then he could have kept it rolled up in his haversack and it would have come in handy in all sorts of ways. Supposing a feller slipped in a shell-hole somewhere (and plenty did, specially round Ypres), he could just have tied one end round his wrist, chucked the other to two blokes on the duckboards and they could easily have pulled him out. Cheap, simple idea. Why didn't I suggest it, you may ask? Well, you didn't suggest things in them days: you just obeyed orders and got on best way you could.

Chapter 7

The Battle of Cambrai

'Yet the first bringer of unwelcome news
Hath but a losing office, and his tongue
Sounds ever after as a sullen bell,
Remembered knolling a departed friend...'

(*Henry IV, Part 2* by William Shakespeare)

On 11 October 1917 the 29th Division turned its back
on Ypres for a while and moved south again to take part
in the Battle of Cambrai in November. This was the first
great battle in history in which tanks were employed on
a large scale.

Nowhere was the fighting hotter than around
Marcoing, Masnières and Crèvecoeur where 88 Brigade
was heavily engaged. Had it not been for the stubborn
resistance of certain units, including the ones fighting in
Bourlon Wood to the north, that victory could have
turned into a disaster. As it was the front settled down
again to the old trench warfare routine and by 6
December the 29th Division were withdrawn to rest area
around Cauroy near Doullens.

But Charlie was not with them. Two days before that
he got his one and only leave.

In late 1917 towards the end of the year we went to
Cambrai. Well, we didn't actually get there, if you take
my meaning, but that was the general idea. We could see
Cambrai clear enough, but the troops didn't get in there
till a long time after. We was robbed at Cambrai.

It started off all right. We had tanks, a lot of tanks, and they went in first. Old Jerry didn't like that at all and a lot of them nipped off. That was just the job. Then the infantry went forward, machine-gunners supporting them. Mind, the old tanks only used to do about three-miles-an-hour flat out and a lot of them broke down, but we were doing all right.

The big crime at Cambrai was we went too far too fast. We didn't get the reinforcements up quick enough. We had no bloomin' support and we couldn't get anything up and Jerry got on to that pretty quick and he got in round behind us. You got to hand it to Jerry. He never missed a trick. But we missed plenty. Cambrai was just one of them.

It started out as a good idea. I heard that they shelled the German lines in front of Arras unmercifully for a week before and he fell for it and rushed troops there thinking we were going to attack from Arras.

Then they got the tanks marshalled all secret and quiet, and that must have taken a bit of doing because they were terrible noisy things. And with old Jerry keeping his eye on Arras he got caught with his trousers down.

We started to move across open country just before dawn – well, no, it must have been a good bit before dawn because we were at the jumping-off points by dawn. It was a miserable night I remember, November 20th, cold and damp – night before my birthday as a matter of fact. Everything went all right to start with. There were a lot of our planes up that day too.

We met resistance at a place called Tercoing or Marcoing, or it might have been Masnières. Private soldiers weren't issued with maps and villages didn't have their names up on signs: matter of fact villages near the front line were usually just heaps of rubble anyway. So, wherever it was, we had a lot of trouble there. The Newfoundlanders were there making the fur fly as usual.

They were a lovely lot of fellers, very generous — give you anything. Gamblers born they were and talk about fighting! They never knew when they were beaten. I'd have loved to have been with that lot; though I was with them on the Somme for a couple of days. The people in Louvencourt where they were billeted thought the world of them. But they didn't half cop a packet at Marcoing (or Masnières or whatever).

Before long we were all copping it. They had a terrible time up north at Bourlon Wood. Jerry soon tumbled to what was what and got his reinforcements back up from Arras p.d.q. We got bloomin' pushed back and damn nearly encircled. When we were falling back we got muddled up with blokes falling back the other way. It was chaos. Good job when darkness came so somebody could do a bit of sorting out. I believe it was the Scots Guards, some Scottish unit anyhow, who saved us: made a gap and we got through. Then the line stabilized again. But it had all started so well. They say they rang the bells in London for a victory and cheered the Byng Boys: they called us that because General Byng was the head of the army there. I never saw *him* of course. But bloomin' Byng Boys! I ask you! We had nobody there behind us, that was what was wrong.

Anyway after the excitement things settled down. Business as usual. But we were short of ammo. So — you've guessed it — 'Ginge knows where the transport lines are. He won't lose 'is way.' Sometimes I was quite sorry I'd got this reputation, and this was one of the times. We went in the dark, of course, but the road back from this little village where the transport was, was open to the German guns and they used to fire on fixed sights along it now and again, so it didn't matter whether it was dark or not. And they used to shell it for good measure.

We got to the village all right and loaded six mules with .303 ammunition. We'd got a sergeant with us —

crafty merchant he was. When we left the safety of this little village he told me he'd got to go back to see if there was any more loads to come. I was in front 'cos I knew the way. So back he goes and we went on. I was on the leeward side of one mule: I let him go slightly to the front so if he got hit at least I'd got a chance to lie flat. We'd gone quite a bit of the way and then it started. One poor devil went down like a log. So I grabs his mule and the rest follers me. If I'd stopped, the rest of us would have been annihilated. We had to go on. The rest of us got there safe enough. When we'd unloaded the mules they'd wait till it was dark again and then they'd take some of the wounded back on them because there was an Advanced Dressing Station in Marcoing (or Tercoing — I still can't remember). They'd carry anything, mules would. And once you'd dropped a load, all you'd got to do was get on his back and let him feel the reins on his neck, and even if you know a short-cut that mule will retrace every step he's taken and he'll take you right back where you've come from. Don't tell me mules are stupid. They are wonderful animals.

Two days before we come out at Cambrai we got warned for leave — when I say we, I mean David Ross and me. You'll be hearing more about Rossie later on. We got a lift to Doullens and entrained there: it wasn't a cattle-truck one, it was a proper train. We were extremely lucky to get straight on the leave boat at Boulogne — passes stamped, straight on the jetty, queue up to get on and away.

When I got to London I went to my sister's and she was very pleased to see me. She worked at a restaurant at the top of the King's Road in Chelsea by Sloane Square, and I used to meet her every evening when she'd finished work and we'd go out together. We went round London to different places but I remember one outing particularly. Across the road from the Victoria Palace there was a cinema where they had a continuous programme. One of the films was a Pathé film gazette showing troops coming out of the Battle of Arras. The camera seemed to be well down past the crossroads where the naughty bit of road was where I found my mule Munchy, but I told my sister that I'd been in that battle and what happened. Seemed funny me sitting there watching it all and telling my sister all about it.

Anyway, when my leave was up I went back to Victoria Station on me own – my sister was at work. I was happy I was by myself because it was a sad sight to see fellers leaving their wives and kids behind and all their relatives. When I got on I got pushed to the back of the carriage because fellers wanted to lean out of the window to say goodbye to their wives and sweethearts. I was happy there was no one to wave me off – better that way, really.

Anyway, the train started off with a jerk eventually and we went knocking on till we got to Dover. There was kitbags and rifles and packs everywhere because everybody come home fully equipped, and there was blokes from all kinds of regiments. I chatted with one and another.

When we finished up at Dover we went to the Dispersal Station: that was a lot of houses round a big square that the Government had commandeered and there were beds on the floor for the blokes to doss down. And there was a big hall, a canteen, all laid out with grub. It was about four o'clock in the afternoon when I got there, so I got a bed and dumped my equipment and went to have tea. We had bread and jam and tea – as much bread and tea as you wanted. So I packed some slices of this ruti in my haversack – it was cut like bloomin' doorsteps. But you never know in the Army when a bit of bread might be very welcome.

After tea we got fell in and marched down to the jetty. Then we halted and we waited; kept on waiting, waiting, waiting. Then a buzz went round over the grape-vine (marvellous thing, the Army's grape-vine) that there was submarines in the Channel. So they marched us back again. I was quite pleased. I had a damn good kip.

Chapter 8

Back Up On The Salient

'We must arise and go:
The world is cold without
And dark and hedged about
With mystery and enmity and doubt,
But we must go
Though yet we do not know
Who called, or what marks we shall leave upon the
snow...'

('The Call' by Charlotte Mew)

At Passchendaele, the Salient was churned up into a bog: constant shelling had destroyed the intricate drainage system that alone kept the land normally under control. Nowhere in that area is the water-table more than one to two feet below the surface. And the physical exhaustion caused by moving at all in this morass robbed the attacks of final effort. British casualties were more than 300,000; German more than 200,000.

Old Charlie could never quite find the words he wanted to describe the Salient. 'It was a muck-heap,' he said once. 'You couldn't begin to imagine what it was like – and I wouldn't really want you to any'ow. It'd upset you. You couldn't call it a desert: they're dry aren't they? People said it was hell – but that's supposed to be hot, and it was bitter, miserable cold there. I never saw none of the top brass getting their lovely shiny boots dirty in that mud – maybe things might've been different if they 'ad. The mud was the worst. That's what it was, it was all just – mud. And the smell!'

So the winter of 1917-18 was much as Charlie expected

it. 'Back to the slime,' as he resignedly put it. It certainly was a scene of complete desolation.

88 Brigade was taken out of the line in February 1918 and went into divisional reserve around Steenvoorde. A lot of their time was occupied with pick and shovel constructing defences to the rear, in some cases fifteen to twenty miles back from Ypres.

Characteristically, Charlie Byrne's main memories of his winter campaigning were of the near-misses when that 'queer luck' of his preserved him, and of the odd amusing incident when he was not in the line.

We crossed the Channel the next day and landed at Boulogne. Then I was told by the RTO that my Brigade was at Langemarck, so I got on a train for Poperinghe. There we got into fours and was marched up to Ypres. When we got up to the old railway crossing I went off to find our transport lines. The blokes all seemed glad to see me and that was very nice.

The next night I got put on ration carrying. While I'd been on leave they'd had an attack or a raid or something and Jerry gave our troops an hour to clear the wounded away. So they must have had a right do round there. I wasn't sorry I'd missed it.

I was lucky all round. Our Brigade came out of the line after that and we went back on rest. We went back miles to a lovely little village and we stopped there for ten days. While we were there I made myself useful in a funny way.

It was like this: we were billeted in the usual old Belgian farm with a big dung heap in the middle of the courtyard and a big barn. We hadn't been there long when I decided to take a wander round and I poked my nose into this barn. In there was a big tub which was about four feet off the ground and about six feet in diameter; the floor of the tub was on a bit of a slope, and at the lowest part there was an outlet with wire gauze on it. The old farmer was in the tub. He had his trousers turned up to his knees. His wife was throwing basketfuls of those old apples in and he was hanging on to a pole in the middle and sort of marking time on the apples so he was crushing them. I take it he was making cider or something. He looked at me and laughed, and I looked at him and laughed. Then I pointed to my chest and I started marking time, meaning to say I'd like to do it too. So his wife brought a bowl of water and a towel and I took my boots and puttees off and washed my feet. While I was doing that two more blokes came in and wanted to know what was going on. When I told them they wanted to help as well. In the finish the old farmer and his wife were chucking baskets of apples in and the three of us were going round and crushing the juice out. It went through this gauze into another vat and then it was sieved again and so on. While we were all marking time, two more blokes looked in and said, 'Blimey, that's a funny parade ground to be marking time on!' And everybody laughed. I absolutely enjoyed myself. The old farmer was delighted. He was getting his work done three times as fast.

The day after, I'd done my various chores in the morning and I was going back to have my dinner and I sees the boys in the house with this old farmer. He had a big jug and he was pouring them drinks out of it. I suppose it was the same sort of stuff we'd been helping to make the day before, only this would have been made previously of course. Blokes were there who hadn't helped at all but the old farmer was so pleased he was pouring wine or cider or whatever it was for everybody. I had a couple of swigs of the stuff, but − blimey! I reckon if you was to put that stuff in the tank of a car you could drive the car with it. It was like 100-octane fuel!

After that we went back up the line. We went back through Ypres − always had to go through there. They was knocking hell out of Ypres, although by then it was just piles of bricks and dust mostly, but still they were pumping shells into it. Lots of dead horses and dead mules in the Square. Poor little donkeys! Wonderful animals they were.

Pigeons was wonderful, too. In the Second War they had better communications – good wireless sets and that sort of thing. But particularly at Ypres they used to use homing pigeons for carrying messages. You couldn't begin to imagine what the terrain was like round Ypres: it was like walking through muddy porridge – some blokes actually drowned in it. So human runners weren't much good. Behind the lines, where there was still some semblance of a road, a bloke would come up on the old motor-bike with a basket on the back. Then a soldier would take the basket on his shoulders and away off up to the front, plodding through the mud with the pigeons safe in the basket. Of course they didn't take them if there was any signs of a gas attack. Then, when you needed to send a really urgent message back, for artillery support or something like that, the officer would write the message and clip it round the bird's leg. Then the man would take the bird in his two hands; the poor little pigeon'd look at him – very bright eyes they 'ave – then he'd be thrown up in the air. They always did a circle and then away. Sometimes Jerry would take a pot shot at them but he usually missed. Some of them fell in the line of duty. One of them got a medal, I believe – it might have been the VC. He come 'ome with 'arf 'is bloomin' leg off.

We had a rough time at Ypres. Everyone had a bloomin' rough time in the Salient. It was no bloody place to be at all. I had a near thing there; going out on relief it was, too. I forget which lot relieved us, but when we come out of the line I made my usual bee-line through the mud till I got to some railway sleepers. Don't get the idea from me saying I made a bee-line that there was anything quick about it. It was slow going. Just as you come out of the line there was an old German pill-box, concrete thing, at the bottom of the duckboards, but to make your way to that for a bit of cover was bloody suicide, because Jerry knew exactly where it was and the dead lay around there all the while – not a healthy spot. Anyway, there'd been some attempt to build a road with railway sleepers up to the wood – or, leastways, the place where the wood had been. So I used to make my way best as I could till I got there. We used to go out in fours and fives. If we'd all gone out together Jerry would've sent a few shells over and got the bloomin' lot. So as each bay got relieved you was off. You'd be told to assemble at a certain point behind the line and the Sergeant would sort it all out then.

My mate and I was together. I knew the way back all right because I'd done it with the rations. We went to the left, down this cobbled road and there were some guns on the right-hand side just poking out of a little wood. It was very early in the morning and pitch dark. Just behind the guns I could see a sort of little glimmer, like a candle. So me and my mate went to have a look and we found there was a little coffee-stall place in this little wood and there were some ladies serving mugs of tea to the troops coming out of the trenches. They were Red Cross or Salvation Army or something. So we got in the queue, and after you'd got your mug of tea there was a little box at the end of the counter with some Woodbines in. So we had this mug of tea – lovely that was – and a fag. Then (I'm ashamed to think of it now really) I went round again. There was a long queue with all sorts of units mixed up – Jocks, artillery fellers, all kinds – and the ladies were very busy. So I got another swig of tea and got another fag.

Then me and my mate went off down the road again feeling quite happy. It was just breaking daylight by then. It was a long straight bit of road and each side of it were dead mules and bits of limbers where they'd been hit the night before, bringing up the rations, and no one had had time to clear up. There were a lot of blokes drifting down this road on their way back out of the line, going to the village where you'd find the Sergeant and answer the roll.

My mate and I were just strolling along, puffing at our fags, when I heard it: this bloody machine-gun. It's an unmistakable sound and when you hear it you don't wait to look about you and ask silly questions. You move. I give my mate a shove and I dived into the ditch at the side of the road. I don't know where my mate went – he went arse over 'ead somewhere the other side. And this bloomin' German aeroplane came straight along the top of this road, blazing along it with his two machine-guns and flattening blokes out everywhere for about three-quarters of a kilo. Then he veered, turned sharp right and back down for another go. Then he was up and away. He must have taken off in the dark, because planes didn't travel at the speed of sound like they do now and the German airfields were well behind their lines. But he knew where that bit of road was all right. He was up and away waggling his wings much as to say, 'Take the change out of that.' He must have caught a couple of hundred blokes coming out of the line: stretcher-bearers were running around everywhere.

Then I sees my mate with his nose just sticking up out of the ditch over the other side. 'You all right, Ginger?' he says. So we goes off down the road, but much quicker this time. We was scared stiff he'd be back. We agreed the coffee-stall ladies would be all right because they were about sixty yards off the road, but it must have given them a fright.

We always reckoned once you was out of the line and 'alfway down that road, you were home and dry. But, as I said to my mate, 'You're not bloody safe anywhere these days!'

Chapter 9

The Finish

'When this bloomin' war is over,
Oh! How happy I shall be.
When I get my civvy clothes on,
No more soldiering for me.'

(Song, 1914-1918)

The spring of 1918 had produced a most serious situation for the Allied armies. With an anxious eye on the build-up of American troops, the German commanders had planned one final desperate offensive to win the war outright. They had been relieved of the pressure on their Eastern Front by the Russian Revolution in 1917 and the eventual collapse of the Russian armies.

The area chosen for attack was the sector held by the British Fifth and Third Armies from the Somme to Cambrai. Right into April the battle rolled forward: some twelve hundred square miles of territory, over ninety thousand prisoners, over a thousand guns and vast quantities of stores fell into German hands.

But their supply-lines across the churned-up Somme battlefields lengthened, communications became more difficult, and casualties mounted. And the offensive, like all offensives before it, clogged and stopped – just short of Amiens.

The next three-and-a-half months were to be anxious ones for the Allies. The Germans mounted other attacks on other parts of the front, but Michael – the code-name for their March offensive – was to be their last success.

In early August the French and British began to move forward again – slowly but surely. They began at Villers

Bretonneux where the German tide had reached its furthest point in April.

The 29th Division had not borne the brunt of the March blows like the divisions of the Third and Fifth Armies. Nevertheless they endured some punishing times around Hazebrouck, Nieppe and Bailleul in the months that followed.

Charlie had little to say about this period except for one remark which concerned General Haig's famous 'backs to the wall' Order of the Day in April 1918. In the latter part it read: 'There must be no retirement. With our backs to the wall and believing in the justice of our cause each one must fight on to the end...' When he heard this piece of inspiring prose, Charlie sniffed derisively. 'Be all right' he commented, 'if there was a bloody wall to put our bloody backs to! Far as I can see there's only fresh air and open French country − not even a decent bloody trench!' However, he picked up his ammunition boxes and, true to his wartime philosophy, continued 'to obey the last order' − wall or no wall.

In September 88 Brigade found themselves in the Ypres area yet again. They were to have more stubborn fighting in October but at least this time they were going in the right direction − it looked as though they might be on their way to Germany at long last.

It almost goes without saying that the final attack began in a downpour. As Charlie Byrne puts it: 'There was plenty of rain around Ypres.' Then, on 11 November, with the brigade at Lessines, the Armistice was signed and the fighting came to an end.

Private Byrne remembers Lessines and its brewery with great relish. It was Lessines that printed the following quaintly welcoming placard: 'Welcome to the Allies Armies. Honour and gratitude to our valourous defenders. Let us glorify our heros. Hourra for the Liberty. Lessines, Le 11 Novembre 1918.'

On 18 November the 29th Division set off for its march into Germany. 'Grub and fags' (Charlie's words) were short all the way because the food supplies for the twenty thousand men depended on one pontoon bridge across the Scheldt and, before that, there was the incredible morass of the old No Man's Land around Ypres to be crossed. The men were filthy, covered with lice and close to exhaustion. The marches were anything up to twenty miles a day over bad roads. The weather was appalling. And as Charlie put it: 'There wasn't much of the conquering 'eroes about us.'

By mid-December, 88 Brigade arrived to take up their positions in the Army of Occupation twenty miles north-east of Cologne. During Christmas 1918 in this area Private Byrne did his own fraternizing; his personal brand of forgiving and forgetting.

Early in 1919 he quitted the Continent and landed in 'Blighty' to announce firmly and thankfully to his family: 'I'm 'ome.'

In late 1918 the 29th Division started moving forward in the Ypres sector. We still had the red triangle up on our shoulders; carried those all the way to Germany. We passed through Hooge Wood. Before we got to that we went past Hell Fire Corner. It was a very famous place, that was − well, a very bad place really. When we marched past it in 1918 it was all right. Jerry was on the run, you see − he wasn't lobbing no shells at that time. But there was a board there that said: 'Don't loiter here'. Someone had got no brains − or a funny sense of humour.

We stopped in Hooge Wood for a rest. Before then you wouldn't have stopped there for a rest: wouldn't have got in the bloody place hardly. There was a tank in there − a derelict. The first mass attack of tanks was at Cambrai in 1917 and very successful it was too. But before that they'd used them a few at a time, sort of in penny numbers. This must have been one of those.

Bloody silly using tanks at Ypres; they just got bogged down in all that mud − pathetic really. This one had a tree-stump stuck up in the middle of the two tracks. I should think it was a casualty from Third Ypres: that's the battle they usually refer to as the Battle of Passchendaele. You know, I don't really remember my war being divided up into these neat packets that they label Battles of This or That. I hear about them with these titles and it's very interesting. But it wasn't like that to us. I suppose everyone realized that First of July was something special, but it fizzled out. Nothing was quite the same after that. But in the main we just kept on keeping on; we obeyed orders and there was carrying parties and wiring parties and things. Shells kept on coming over. Then they'd start making big dumps of ammo and stuff, and the Medical Corps fellers'd be extra busy with piles of bandages and what-not – then we'd know there was an extra bit of nastiness on the way. You'd get what were called latrine rumours, that is to say a lot of soldiers' gossip about what was coming off. Really wild some of those were; mind, there was a lot of truth in some of them too.

Anyway – this tank in Hooge Wood: the crew were still in it. You could see one feller still sitting there slumped forward and his one arm flung out. I don't know why I did it but I touched his arm as if I wanted to attract his attention and there was nothing there. You would have thought his arm was there because the sleeve was still the same shape, but there was nothing there. It did feel queer. I went off after my mates. After we'd gone through Hooge we kept on keeping on. I forget the names of the villages. They were strange to us in any case because they'd always been behind the German lines up to then. Most of them were messed up and the roads were in a shocking state. First thing I saw German was an old field-cooker that had been captured with the six mules in it, and the mules had their numbers tatooed on their lips.

Anyway, we finally got to a place called Lessines and we stopped there for ten days. And that's where I ended my war, that's where I was when the Armistice was declared. They said we were going to Germany and the order came round that anybody reporting sick would be sent to the Base. Anybody who'd got sore feet or bad legs and felt they couldn't stand up to a gruelling march were to report sick. We didn't much like the sound of that 'gruelling march' but I said to my mate, 'I'm going to bloody well see it out now.'

'So am I,' my mate said. 'After all this time I'm going to get to Germany, I am. If it's the last thing I do I'll get fell in.'

It wasn't that we got bad legs or anything, but we'd both got terrible thick heads! You'll laugh at this; when we got to Lessines it was like a soldier's dream of Paradise, because our section was lucky enough to stop in a brewery. And it was in full working order. The people there treated us lovely. They had no food, of course – just behind the lines they were carting off all the dead horses and mules to eat. Horse flesh is all right to eat, but some of them old mules was a bit bloody tough, I bet. Think of my little Munchy who'd been through the South African War! But the Belgians were very nice to us. They didn't like the Germans – if they saw some prisoners they'd throw stones at them or try to get at them and slosh them. There was an old Belgian feller in this brewery; he couldn't speak English; he used to work in the room where they barrelled the beer and there was a line of mugs hung up there. He made us understand we could use any of them except one particular one because that was his. But think of it! Ten days in a brewery!

All good things come to an end. Off we went to Cologne, ten days' march behind the Germans. We was cold and tired. We weren't fighting of course, but it was a damned long way, and the lads were foot-slogging every yard of it. I didn't march all the way because sometimes I was on transport. When a bloke got tired another bloke would take his rifle off him for a bit to give him a bit of a lift. Sometimes we'd try and sing. But there wasn't much of the conquering 'eroes about us. One day I was following the front section with the transport on a mule. In some ways you was better off marching — you got to feeling like a bloody brass monkey stuck out there in the cold sitting up there on the blinkin' donkey. Only thing was you didn't have to carry a pack — transport fellers' packs was on the limbers. Anyways, I sees this bloke in the front section was looking a bit tired, a bit ribby, so at the next halt I said to the old Sergeant, 'Can I give that bloke a break, he looks rough.' The Sergeant agreed. So I told this feller to give me his rifle and get on the mule a bit to rest his legs. He didn't have to do anything, just sit on it. So I had his rifle and my own and I took his place in the front section of fours, second man. These rifles weighed eight pounds each, you know, or maybe a bit more than that.

The officer was just ahead on his charger — that's what they called the officers' horses but they couldn't have charged anything, they was so knackered up. It was switching its tail and we were going up a bit of a hill. I'd got my own rifle over one shoulder and this other rifle over the other shoulder, and I had a bright idea. I leant forward and got hold of the horse's tail; not to pull it, you understand, but to sort of kid myself mentally it was helping me up the hill. Then the Sergeant yelled, 'Let go of that horse's tail!' And the officer he turned round and he soon sized up what was going on. 'Leave the man alone, Sergeant,' he says. 'Can't you see he's carrying two rifles?' So that was all right; but when we got to our destination that Sergeant got a right telling-off from the boys about screaming his head off and stamping his feet on parade. 'Make you carry two bloody rifles tomorrow and see how you like it,' they said to him.

Being on the transport wasn't no picnic either. When the boys had finished their day's march they just had to go into the billets the officers found and then it was 'Eyes down, look in', make way for the old field-cooker to come up. He had six mules on to make sure he got there. Then all they had to do was rest, have their food, and do what they liked. It was bitter cold winter weather.

But on the transport we had to find a place for the animals and then water them. Then it was feed-up time and you had to stop there till they'd finished and take their nose-bags off. We didn't usually manage to get our food until about two hours after we'd reached our destination because the animals always had to be seen to first. The only thing was you didn't have to carry your pack in the transport. But otherwise it just seemed to be work, work, work.

We'd been going about five or six days I suppose when I had a bit of luck. Lieutenant Layton was put on Billeting Officer and he had to have a groom with him and I got the job. I dossed down in the transport lines the night before because we had to be away very early. The picket — that's a sort of sentry put out to look after the animals — came round and knocked me on the ankle to wake me up. I got a canteen of tea and some biscuits and we was ready for the off.

The officer had a horse, of course, with a bag of oats tied on the back to give him a feed later on. Me, I had a mule. I couldn't get on this bloomin' mule with my equipment and my bloomin' rifle, so I says to the officer, ''Ere, hold this will you, please.' He was that flummoxed he took it, and he just said, 'Come on, come on. We haven't got all night, you know.' So I got myself up on the mule somehow, and he handed me my rifle back and I slung it round me over my pack. It was pitch dark. No street lights nor nothing. The officer had a torch and his map used to hang round his neck with a sort of cellophane cover thing on it.

It was a bit of a job making that mule keep up with the horse but we managed all right. I enjoyed it. When it came daylight you should have seen the welcome we got from the villages we went through. Some of the people even had little Union Jacks. I don't remember any of the names of these villages — don't suppose I ever knew them really. We went through a place called Spa. The officer told me that was what it was called. When we got to the border of Germany the Lieutenant said something to some fellers standing in front of a gate. I don't know what he said — he could speak German. But they all stood to attention when he spoke to them, and they were at attention as we rode by. There was me on this blinkin' donkey, feeling like Napoleon crossing the Alps — or maybe that was Hannibal.

I enjoyed that ride; gave me poor tired old 'dads' a bit of a rest. I got a smashing billet too — it was in a granary where there was water running by and a big wheel for the grindstones to make flour for the bread. This German lady gave me her son's bedroom. Her son had got killed in a submarine. She had photographs of him and of his submarine. There was a lovely bed with white sheets and all, but I didn't sleep in that. She thought I did, but I didn't. I just tossed the blankets about and then lay down on the floor and put my overcoat on top of me and had a good kip on the deck. I'd slept in worse places. I couldn't sleep in that lovely bed because I was bloomin' lousy, see. And she had been kind to me.

Out on the main road there was a coffee stall some society or other in England had set up to give tea and stuff to prisoners who had been captured during the war who were marching back from Germany. Of course there was nobody there when we got there. Earlier on, when we were moving up from Lessines, we'd passed quite a few of these fellers — they all had a big broad stripe down their trousers and I wondered who they were at first. We used to wave at them and say, 'What divvy, mates?' And they'd wave back and shout to us and after the first day we knew what they were. Don't know where they came from, but they were making their way back. I suppose when the war was over the Germans had opened the cages and told them to bugger off. But some of the poor blighters looked as though they'd travelled a long way. They'd get no bloomin' medals.

Best camp we had was at a place called Elsenborn — that was in Germany. It was a big military barracks. There was a nice large square in front with horse-troughs, and the barrack-rooms were on top of the stables. No Jerries, of course. But he was a wise old bird was Jerry, putting the rooms over the stables because the heat of the animals gave the rooms some warmth. There was no beds there, just bare boards, but it was dry and it wasn't too bad. But we only stopped there the one night and then we were away again.

I think it must have been about three nights after that we stopped at a big brick kiln. It wasn't far from Cologne. They said we were going to have a day's rest there. Then the order come round that we had to clean all the brass on our equipment. Fancy 'bulling' blokes like that when they'd marched all that way! Actually it was quite simple really because there was this brick dust everywhere. All you had to do was bend down with a bit of wet sand-bag, rub the brass with it, let it dry, then polish it up and it come up all right. Some of them even cleaned the back of the brasses. I didn't. I cleaned the front — the part that showed.

So everybody was spick and span and everything in apple-pie order for the march across the Rhine bridge. I had a grandstand view, being on the back of a mule. But then we came to this circle of top brass — top brass being generals and such like — and at the back of them was their flunkeys (I suppose you'd call them ay-dee-camps) and they'd got those lances stuck in their stirrups with the little flags on top. But you ought to have seen the medals they had on their chests! They couldn't get any more on. They were absolutely smothered in 'em. And there was all the blokes saying, 'Look at that bloody shower! Where'd you get your medals then? Bloody shower!' And the old Sergeant saying, 'Quiet lads, steady lads.' What a proper blinkin' pantomime! They must have heard, there's no question about it. I had to laugh.

So over the Rhine bridge we goes – I don't know the name of it. Mid-December it would be. We stopped in a big granary after that for about three days. Then they bunged us out to a little village about thirty-five kilometres the other side – ever such a tiny village: I think it was called Dammerhausen. That's where I spent my Christmas in 1918. We had a halt just before we got to the village when we were marching in and I spotted a gateway leading down to a little farm. And I had a bright idea.

One of the Australian artillerymen I knew had given me a two-ounce packet of tobacco with a gold label on the front. You could chew it if you wanted. But I smoked fags and I'd had this packet in my pocket for about six months. So I thought I'll give old Jerry a present. Well, it was Christmas Eve and we'd been heaving quite different sorts of presents at each other for the previous four Christmases, hadn't we?

So off I trudged through the snow. I went by myself, because if it turned out to be a little old lady by herself she might've been frightened if there'd been more than one soldier. I opened the gate and walked down the footpath and knocked on the door. An old German with one of those big pipes opened the door and he just looked at me. I didn't know any German except 'Gut morgen' so I said that. Then I took this packet of baccy out of my pocket and offered it to him, and I held out my hand. So we shook hands. Then he stood back and motioned me to go inside.

His wife was there and his two sons. They all welcomed me and we all shook hands. They didn't have much food, but they had a good fire and we all sat round the fire. The language barrier was terrible, but we tried speaking to each other in what bit of French we had. The old lady obviously couldn't understand anything. The two sons gave me to understand they'd been machine-gunners in the German army. I said I'd been a machine-gunner too and we all nodded our heads. It was a pity I'd no German and they couldn't speak English hardly; we could have had a nice professional chat, being all in the same trade as you might say. I wondered afterwards if either of them could have been that gunner on the Somme in 1916. I'd willingly have shaken him by the hand; he knew his job all right.

But I knew my job, too, and I knew what he was up to. Looking back I had to laugh; I bet he said to himself, 'Where did that bugger get to?'

I'd spotted a little accordion on one of the kitchen shelves; it had three tremblers on the top. So I pointed to it and the old farmer got it down and gave it to me. I played 'Silent Night' and they sang it in German and I sang it in English. They really loved that. We enjoyed it so much, we sang it twice. Their national anthem is one of our hymn tunes, you know. I learned all the words of the German national anthem when I was in school — in English, of course. In those days they were sort of relations of ours; still are, I suppose; kind of cousins. Our kings and queens have German ancestors. Funny, really.

I never saw them again, that German farmer and his family. I was due for leave shortly after. There were four of us — one was David Ross; he had the MM. Don't know what he got it for. He always said it come up with the rations. Anyway we marched off down to this dispersal camp. There were an awful lot of 'red-caps' there (military policemen). There was a big square, like a prison yard it was, and we were all lined up there; they'd picked out different blokes to go in front of the doctor. I was unlucky. I got picked on. When I got to this doctor he asked if I was clean; if I'd got any lice. There's a silly question! Everyone was lousy. But I says, 'No, sir.' Anyway he made me take my clothes off and he looks through a magnifying glass and then says, sarcastic-like, 'No lice, eh? What are those then? Butterflies? Go back and get yourself de-loused.' He had a funny Yankee accent, and I could have kicked him in the teeth. So I went back to the village where I'd come from and I found a German lady with an iron. She ironed all the seams on my clothes with a very hot iron. It doesn't finally get rid of them usually − lice and rats is the only born survivors in war. But it was good enough to qualify me, so I went back the next day. This time I didn't get called out.

We took a civilian train to Cologne. When I got there I found I hadn't lost any time because I caught the others up. Some blokes had been hanging around on that platform for twelve days waiting for the leave train. You see they had to lay the lines over the old No Man's Land back in Flanders to connect up and they had problems. I was two days on that bloody platform and I wasn't very big: being small has its advantages but you do get pushed around. But in the end comes this great big steam engine, clouds of smoke, dragging a very long train with a big golden German eagle on each carriage and a dab of whitewash over the eagle. I would have laughed about that under other circumstances, but when it pulled in there was such a free-for-all to get on. You never saw anything like it! What with your pack and your rifle and bits and pieces! Some blokes had spurs on! Cor! I did fight my way into a carriage and I couldn't bloody well stand up. Leave train or no leave train I was sorry I'd bloomin' got on.

It took about two days to get from Cologne to Le Havre. You had to go very, very slowly where the plate-layers were joining the track together. Then it would pick up steam again, then stop again. It stopped outside one railway station; I forget the name of the place but it was in France. We could see people walking along a road by a wire fence and the station was just down the track. One of my mates said, 'Blow this! I ain't having no more of it,' and he opened the door and jumped down on to the track. Three of us got out and one feller stayed behind.

We found a café and had some biscuits and some vin blanc. Then we got to the station and we found a French interpreter. They wore big caps and had coloured arm-bands to show which language they spoke. David Ross had a thick Scots accent, so old Fred Marsh who came from London said, 'Don't you speak to him, Rossie. I can't bloomin' well understand half you say, leave alone 'im.' So we went along to the interpreter and Fred told him we'd come from Cologne and was trying to make our way to Le Havre.

'From Cologne?' says this Frenchman. 'You *have* had a long walk!'

'Didn't bloody walk,' said Fred, 'got off that train up the line, there.'

Well, he'd guessed that, of course, so he just smiled and took us round to the station-master and put things right with him. He told us to stop on the platform because there'd be a train to Le Havre along soon. We'd lost all the others. Talk about wanderin' bloody minstrels! I thought to meself.

This train finally came in and it was full of French sailors. But they made room for us and shook hands. Everyone was trying to talk at once, saying where they'd come from and where they'd bin. They were as happy as sandboys. It was all over, see. No one wasn't going up the line, not never again. Everyone was merry and bright.

We got to Le Havre all right and when we'd tumbled out, who was the first person we should meet but one of those bloomin' red-caps. The place was swarming with them.

'Where do you think you're going?' he says.

'Bloody Blighty, I 'ope,' answers Rossie. 'I've been out 'ere long enough.'

So the red-cap asked to see our passes. When he'd looked at them he said, 'That train didn't come from Cologne.' Right nasty suspicious lot red-caps are. Rossie come right back at him. 'Don't care a damn where the bloomin' train come from. *We* did.' He could be a rough character could Davie, and I don't think that red-cap liked the look of him, so he marched us all down to the RTO (Rail Transport Officer).

When we got there we let Ross do the talking because he'd got the MM up and all. He gave the officer the full strength; told him all our little troubles. He listened. Then he turned to the red-cap and said he didn't think it was necessary to take us up to the dispersal camp and would the red-cap please see us down to the jetty.

'Yes,' he says, a bit grim, 'I'll see them down to the jetty, Sir.'

Nothing'd stop Rossie once he got started. He turned round. 'You take us down to the jetty and put us on the leave-boat,' he says, 'and I'll take back everything I ever said about red-caps.'

We 'ad a right quiet walk down to the jetty, I can tell you.

We had to wait there till it was our turn to get in the queue to give the Embarkation Officer our papers, because there was a lot of paperwork to do. The boat was in but it was getting loaded; and the queue shuffled round, round, all round until we get up the gang-plank and then we were off – over to Blighty. That was my finish with Germany.

When we got to Victoria we decided we couldn't go home as we were all lousy as could be. So we asked a couple of red-caps what we ought to do. I saw more red-caps in that last week than I'd seen the rest of the war put together. They didn't get up to the front much, see. Anyway, they marched us off down to Wellington Barracks.

This bloomin' Guardsman Sergeant-Major there looked at us as much as to say, 'Soldiers! Bloody fine soldiers you are, ain't you?' There was me with a dirty cap-badge, and gas-mask slung over one shoulder. But he didn't say nothing. They marched us to the baths, drew chalk rings round us and made us leave our clothes there. Then we had a lovely bath and they put some special liquid on us, washed our 'air, good sluice down. Then we dried ourselves. After that we were given clean pants, socks, vest, shirt; the next thing was khaki trousers and tunic. Well, this was the Guards and I'm not a big feller; everything was too big for me. I looked a right Charlie, if you'll forgive the pun.

But I was nice and clean, so I got my equipment, walked down the King's Road and went to see my sister. I walked in the door there and they said, 'Cor blimey, where've you come from?'

'I'm 'ome,' I said.

Chapter 10

A Land Fit For Heroes

'Anythin' for a quiet life, as the man said wen he took the sitivation at the light-house.'

(*The Pickwick Papers* by Charles Dickens)

Well, I might have been home but I wasn't out of the wood, not by a long chalk. I was still in the Army and bloomin' fed up with it, too. It was 1919 and we'd won the war, hadn't we? I wasn't trained for nothing except firing machine-guns and looking after them. I was good at that mind, but I couldn't see much future in it at the time. As I told you I'd been apprenticed as a blacksmith's striker before I joined up but I didn't fancy going back to that.

Anyway, my sister was friendly with a Frenchwoman and she 'ad a taxi-service in London. I'd run odd errands for her and done a few odd jobs in the past. So she writes me a letter to say she'd employed me before the war (which she 'adn't) and she was willing to employ me again on getting my discharge (which she wasn't − I knew that − she'd got enough blokes working for her). Only there was an order came out that if you could get your old job back you could apply for your discharge from the Army. I suppose it wasn't the right thing to do really, but other blokes was getting out and I couldn't see me getting my discharge, so I thought I'd better use my loaf and look about me sharpish.

So I took this letter to the RTO. He sends me to the

Machine Gun Corps Pay Office at Chelsea. Then I got orders to report to the Crystal Palace. Off I goes. I went in to the Crystal Palace a soldier with my rifle and equipment and everything on, and I come out the other end a civvy — civvy clothes, civvy suit. And I drew thirty-five quid blood money — that's me gratuity, see. Then I was on me own. Out of the Army and out of a job.

Anyway this lady who'd written me the letter, she was very kind to me. Her husband had been a bus-driver and he'd had a friend who knew a man who used to take 'em on at the training-school at the bus depot. She was sympathetic because I'd been a soldier, so she wrote another letter for me to give this bloke down at Milman's Street in Chelsea.

So the next day early I goes down. There was hundreds of blokes waiting outside looking for work. But I gave the bloke at the wicket-gate my letter and he comes back in a little while and tells me to step inside. Then I saw an interviewing officer and then on to a doctor who passed me fit.

Then I 'ad to go to school — with seats and the old blackboard — to be trained as a conductor on the old LGOC, the London General Omnibus Company. There was a sort of schoolmaster and he put sums up on the blackboard. There was ha'penny, penny, twopenny, threepenny tickets and so on up to about one and twopence — that was in the old proper money of course (I've never got used to this new money myself). You'd have clips of each sort of ticket and there was 50 to a clip: let's take the penny ones — they started at 00000 — so when you got to 0049 you knew you'd sold 50 tickets, 4s. 2d. worth. Simple really. You'd add it all up and put it on your way-bill. Then you made sure the numbers follered on when you put in a new clip. This schoolmaster was putting up sums to do with all the various kinds of tickets. I passed with flying colours. Some of the blokes couldn't do it at all so they didn't get a job. I passed all right. Before he'd finished writing them out I had the answer in me 'ead, before I even got the paper to write it down. My army school had grounded me well in arithmetic. The old Sergeant had an ebony ruler and one of those canes with a curl on the end – 'e used to give you a right fourpenny one if 'e thought you was lazy. And when you got your homework you didn't go out to play till it was finished, I tell you.

So I'm grateful because I passed my tests all right. Then I had ten days at two bob a day as a learner, just going around learning the routes. Then the day came when you got your own punch and you had an inspector with you for a bit. You'd pick up your first passengers. Help them on. Don't ring the bell till they're sat down. Then ding-ding. The old driver knew he had a learner behind him so 'e'd move off gentle, see. 'Fares please.' Then you'd punch the ticket, got to punch it in the right place. Give 'em the change. The bloomin' bags to put the money in were so tight they used to take the quick off your fingers nearly.

The day soon came when I was on me own. I was put on the bloomin' 24 route from Ebury Bridge to Camden Town. Belting down the Tottenham Court Road I didn't know where I was – never been there before in me life. What a bloomin' joke! But I soon learned. I had a miserable driver: he couldn't keep up with the bloke in front. The further away you got from the bus in front the more passengers you'd pick up and the busier the conductor would be. If there's three buses close up, you making a fourth, you'd pull up at a stop, everybody's gone – ding-ding and away you go. That's the reason buses in London come like blinkin' bananas – in bunches. It didn't matter how much money you took, you didn't get any bonuses. As long as you worked the schedules that was all right.

At first I had to go from one garage to another but, after a time, you'd graduate to having your own driver at one particular garage. Then you'd just look at your schedules, see what you'd got to do, see when your days off were. It wasn't too bad at all.

Sometimes you had a hard road, sometimes you had an easy one — but that's life isn't it? Like the old 84 route from Golders Green was easy. I used to like the East End best. The Lascar seamen and the old Cockney women they'd cuss and swear at you, but that was all. But if you got round to Mill Hill and Harrow where the posh folk lived they'd report you if you moved off two seconds before you was due: if you were reported you were inside the office — three of those and it was the sack.

It wasn't a bad life on the buses. Bit hard on the feet, but you got used to it. Not as bad as soldiering anyways. But in 1929 I got appendicitis — got it bad. I had to have it out and when I come out of hospital they said I wouldn't be able to work on the buses any more — too much standing. So that was that.

Life wasn't easy in the thirties. There wasn't a lot of work about but I made out: did a bit here and a bit there. Worked the markets for a while. Quite hard work that was, especially in bad weather but I had a few laughs and somehow made ends meet. Then along comes another war. As though we hadn't had enough with the first one. Mind, the fourteen—eighteen do was a bit of a surprise really. 'It'll be all over by Christmas,' they said. But you could see the second one coming a mile off. Had to do something about that Hitler. And we knew that one wasn't going to be over in five minutes. People said it wasn't another war at all — just a continuation of my little lot: apparently we didn't finish it off properly — though we thought we 'ad. War to end wars that was. What I shudder to think about is if some crazy bugger in Africa or Asia or the Middle East or somewhere sounds off and starts number three. Don't want my grandchildren and yours to 'ave to do what we 'ad to. Anyways, I'm an optimist. Maybe we have all learned something: all those big cemeteries in France and Belgium — they couldn't have died for just nothing, could they?

Oh, I knew there was a couple of things I was going to tell you about.

Remember me telling you about my mate, Ted Smith — the one who lost his arm in 1916? Well, funny thing — I was with him when he died. That was years afterwards. My brother who played the drums in the Regimental Band went into Chelsea Hospital after his wife died and I used to go and see him. One day he said to me, 'Remember old Ted Smith? He's in the hospital ward. He's not at all well. Don't know anybody.' So I went up to see him. I told the nurse who I was and how I'd been with him when he lost his arm in the war, and she said she didn't think I'd get any sense out of him but I could try if I liked. So I sat down by his bed. He was sort of half asleep, so I shook him gently. 'Ted,' I says. 'Ted. It's me, Ginger.'

He tipped his head to one side. 'Ginger. Ginger. What, old Ginge?' Bright as you please.

'Yes, old Ginger. Do you remember when you was at Beaumont-Hamel and had your blinkin' arm off?'

'Course I bloody do,' he says. Then he was quiet for a long time.

So I try again. 'What's your number, Ted?'

'Forty-one twenty.'

'What's my number?'

'Forty-one twenty-four. How are you getting on, Ginge?'

I was pleased. 'I'm doing all right. So you've still got your noddle screwed on, then? Why don't you get up and walk about a bit, Ted?' But he didn't answer. I shook him. Then I tried again but I couldn't get a word out of him after that. After a long while I looks up, and there's a doctor in a white coat standing there. 'I'm afraid he's just given up,' he says. Poor old Ted!

The other thing was about that brooch I picked up in Ypres Cathedral. I always meant to take it back. Well, my son Charlie was a keen amateur footballer and his team was organized to go over and play some little village team in Belgium. So we were all going over to watch this match, and we all put in for passports. Young Charlie got his, his wife got hers, everybody got theirs but I didn't.

So I rang up the passport office in London. The bloke on the other end of the line says, 'Ho, yes! I've got your application here. But you were born in Dublin, weren't you? That makes you an alien.' I exploded. 'What do you mean, a bloody alien? I went right through the 1914–1918 War, didn't I? Anyway do I talk like a bloomin' Mick?' He had to admit that I didn't and said he'd try and cut through some red tape for me. The upshot was that I had a letter from the St Albans police station stating that if I would swear allegiance to the Queen, then they'd give me my passport. What a carry-on!

I only got it two days before we were due to go. Then I thought about the brooch. I always used to wear it pinned behind the lapel of an old coat I had. I couldn't find this coat anywhere, so I said to the wife, 'Where's that old coat, Ada?'

'Oh, that,' she said, 'I got fed up seeing that old thing hanging about, so I slung it in the rag-bag.'

'Where's the rag-bag, then?'

'Rag-man come and collected it last week.' She was that bloomin' tidy and methodical was my Ada. So away went the bloomin' brooch. Pity really, I'd have liked to have taken it back where it came from.

Envoi

Sixty-Two Years Later

Mr Byrne did go back to Beaumont-Hamel, but not until 1978. He had not forgotten in the intervening years all that happened on that now-so-quiet stretch of French countryside. He had an absorbingly interesting couple of days, it seems. Unfortunately it was not possible to tape his personal reactions. Arrangements were made to do this, but his sudden death prevented it.

His son, Charlie Junior, kindly agreed to record his own recollections of the occasion. The resultant chapter details what old Mr Byrne did, and faithfully reflects his emotions on that sentimental journey. Given that father and son understood each other so well, this account is probably very close indeed to the tape that Old Charlie himself might have made.

Charlie Byrne left behind many friends. For he bore no malice and 'the whole world was his friend'.

All my life Pop has talked about the 1914–1918 War – which is understandable. I grew up with the name Beaumont-Hamel, which meant nothing to me but obviously meant something very special to him. It wasn't really until the latter years of his life that we talked a lot about the First World War and I began to realize just how important Beaumont-Hamel was.

My mother died in July 1976 and Pop was really down after that: I had quite a few problems trying to get him interested in life again. One day he mentioned Beaumont-Hamel and I had an idea. I said, 'Why don't we go there? Why not go back, Pop? I'll come with you. I'd like to go.' And I honestly did want to go; I was curious about the place, I'd heard so much about it. He hesitated for a long time. I said, 'Come on, Pop. I don't know quite what we'll see when we get there or who we'll meet, but we'll just take it as it comes.' That suited Pop all right: that was his philosophy of life — take it as it comes. So we arranged to be there on 1 July 1978.

I remember as we were going down to Albert we could see the sun shining on the Golden Virgin, slightly to the right-hand side. Pop remarked on it. We got into Albert about midday and decided we'd have a couple of beers in a café. In his usual friendly style Pop tried to talk to the few people in there, but they didn't understand any English — couldn't get any sense out of them. Then he pointed to the red triangle on his shoulder and said, 'Beaumont-Hamel.' Then their faces lit up and they nodded and smiled, 'Ah! Beaumont-Hamel!' and pointed down the road.

So away we went. Just before we got to the line of trees bordering the [Newfoundland] Park we looked down on a sunken road on the right and Pop said to me, 'I wonder if that's the sunken road I've told you about. It bloody could be.'

When we got into the Park we enquired of the French gardener for the Warden, Mr Steve Austin. He spoke limited English, but he made us understand Mr Austin would not be there until the next day, so we arranged to meet him at nine-thirty the next morning. Then we walked up towards the big Caribou memorial. Pop pointed to the trenches and No Man's Land: 'There it is,' he said, 'there it all is.' Just then a young lady (whose name we found out later was Sue Cox) came up and asked Pop if he knew anything about the place. He replied, characteristically, that he bloody well should do; he was there in 1916. She was delighted and they set off talking ten-to-the-dozen.

So I left them to it. I wandered off on my own. I looked around and I tried to imagine what it had been like, but I couldn't. It's hard to explain. The sun was shining and it was all so nice and peaceful. There were the trenches and the shell-holes all right, but there was lovely green grass growing in them. There were two pretty cemeteries with white crosses in the far corners and trees all round the edge. It was all so neat and quiet. I dunno, I thought to myself, this is the place Pop came to see. This is the place I came to see, but – it looks so *tranquil*! I stood looking down into the trenches and then it struck me. Somebody had made them; somebody had dug those trenches. People had lived in them – and died in them too. Pop had been in those very trenches I was looking at. And then it really began to come to me.

After a while I went back to him. He was still talking to Sue Cox. She had to go but said she'd be there the next morning. So Pop and I went for a wander round the Park. He was full of it. He looked out over No Man's Land, looked at this and looked at that. You could see he was really taken up with it. I had to drag him away in the end.

I'm pleased that Pop went back to Beaumont-Hamel in 1978 because it was obvious he really wanted to go. It wasn't all happiness, of course; he had a little sniffle when he was in the Park at the wreath-laying ceremony, but it was only to be expected and he got over it all right.

Talking about the wreath-laying ceremony, that made him so proud. And I was proud of him because he did it so well. I was really proud; he did it in proper Army fashion – upright and soldierly. I know for sure he was deeply touched; very deeply. He told me afterwards that when he and Steve Austin had laid the wreaths, they stood together for a moment and then he murmured quietly to Steve, 'Poor bastards!' And Steve replied, 'How right you are, Charlie.' Whether they were the right words to say or the wrong words to say on such an occasion I don't know, but that's exactly what Pop did say. And he meant it – the way he always meant things.

He was so proud to be asked to lay the wreaths. He was surprised when Steve Austin asked him to do it; there was no rehearsal or anything like that, but he did it absolutely right. In the car afterwards he said to me, 'Think of that! Me, a plain bloody private, laid them wreaths. It's always been generals and colonels laying wreaths before. But this time they asked an ordinary plain bloomin' private.' He was very struck with that; he mentioned it to me several times afterwards.

But the trip wasn't all solemnity. We had a lot of laughs; a lot of fun. He could be right obstinate sometimes. Well, he'd had his rest on the Saturday afternoon and when he got up he decided he wanted a paper. 'I'll just pop out and get a *Sun*,' he said.

'They won't sell the *Sun* here, Pop,' I told him. But he wasn't having that. 'Course they will,' he insisted. 'They were selling 'em in Calais.' The idea that anywhere could be so benighted as not to sell the *Sun*– even a little very French place like Albert – he wasn't going to entertain. So I gave up and off he went. Sure enough he came back after a while looking rather sheepish. 'Get your paper, Pop?' I enquired. 'Don't bloody sell 'em,' he grunted.

Another thing that we often laughed about afterwards, Pop and I did, was an incident before we got to bed on the Sunday night. We'd had quite a few drinks and quite a merry night. Pop was well oiled; well away. When we got into our double room in the early hours I stood him up in a corner and I said, 'Little man, you've had a busy day!' And he looked at me and grinned. 'Yes,' he said, 'but a bloody good 'un.' That was Pop! One of his sayings, his motto – and he really lived up to it right to the very end – was 'You only pass this way once. So while you do, give it a bloody good hammering.' And he exactly lived up to those words.

Another memory of him was when we were looking around the Park the first day. He was talking about various things and he asked the French gardener where Englebelmer was. The man pointed it out to him behind some trees. Sue Cox was with us at the time and, after he died, she sent me a poem that she'd written. It's very good because it's exactly the way he said this particular thing at that moment:

'Where's Englebelmer?' he asked the guide.
'Over there below the rise,'
The Frenchman gestured to curved hill-side.
'We slept there then behind the guns,'
He said as turned to gaze, and sighed,
Hearing again the boots and songs.
'And there the Front Line,' the man replied.
'No, it's not. It's over one more.
I was there — it's the signs have lied!'
And this white-haired old soldier
Stood straight on the cairn and gently cried.
'There the stark, dark Tree of Death
That gave no shelter from bullets that scythed
Through hearts and heads of boys
Who journeyed to France and fought and died.'
All the while, through his words,
The horrors of war were specified
For those who stood and heard.
In them he instilled such warmth and pride,
A survivor who now returned.

It was a perfect trip — lovely weekend; no problems. Pop sat beside me pretty quiet most of the way; couldn't tell what he was thinking. But when we got home all he could talk about was his trip to Beaumont-Hamel. It was never his trip to the Somme, always the trip to Beaumont-Hamel. First of July 1916 had made a lasting impression on him that went right through his life. And there was no doubt where his admiration lay: it wasn't the Hampshires he spoke about, it was the Newfoundlanders. 'They were great,' he used to say, 'really great!' I'm truly glad now that I persuaded him to go back. He saw his sunken road and other places that meant a lot to him. The place was quite different from what he remembered, of course − beautiful and peaceful − but I think that made him happy too.

His very sudden death about seven months afterwards really knocked me sideways. It was some comfort to think that it was the way he would have wanted to go − quickly and quietly without fuss. Another comfort was the realization of how many friends he had. They came to the funeral; sent flowers and letters.

One card read: 'Thus has a final battle been fought and a last enemy conquered. Farewell, old friend. Be now at peace, together with your comrades. "At the going down of the sun..." '

Appendix I

Reports on German Gas Attack on Night 8/9 August 1916

(1) Gas helmets were in all cases put on. There was plenty of warning given, so that the helmets were all properly adjusted. The helmets of the Battalions affected were all inspected on the morning of the day of the gas discharge, and were found in good order.

(2) After full enquiries, the course of events appears to have been as follows:-

At about 10.30 p.m. the gas alarm was sounded on my left by the Royal Inniskilling Fusiliers, and taken up by the Hampshire Regiment, who at once put on their helmets. As the alarm was given on the left gas could be heard being emitted directly in front of the Hants Regiment, which began to reach their trenches in a minute or two. This cloud lasted for about twenty minutes. There was a pause during which no helmets were removed. After about ten minutes another gas cloud came over, this time from a half left direction, which also appeared to last about twenty minutes. No further gas was emitted after 11.20 p.m. There had been a few cases of gassing during this time, but not a large number. The Vermorel Sprayers were used to clear the trenches and dug-outs. At about twelve midnight or shortly after, as no gas was apparent in the air, helmets were permitted to be raised and kept rolled up on the head. The men were all standing on the fire-step as high as possible, and a steady fire was being kept up on the enemy. It was after this time that casualties from the gas began to be heavy.

Men, who had apparently been perfectly well, suddenly began to collapse. These casualties continued to occur right up to after midday of the following day.

The men were wearing P.H. helmets and most of the officers P.H.G. The proportion of casualties seems to be about the same with either class of helmet.

The conclusions I have come to are:

(1) The helmets did not give complete protection, owing to the gas cloud being stronger than hitherto experienced. It is impossible for me to say whether there was any new element in the gas used. More probably, the proportions of the Chlorine and Phosgene were different, there being more of the latter gas.

(2) It is of the utmost importance that men should keep quiet long after the gas has gone over. No men should be allowed to walk back to the Dressing Station.

(3) Probably helmets were raised too soon, while gas was still about. There is a borrow trench in front of our trench, and it is possible that gas remained in this. After the cloud passed over, the wind increased in strength, which may have caused the gas in the borrow trench to blow over.

In one part of the line, this trench was sprayed, but there is no evidence that casualties were less in this part of the line.

(4) Men slightly gassed who were lying out behind the trench appeared to be going on well till the sun rose. As the heat of the sun increased they rapidly collapsed, and in most cases died.

(5) Ammonia administered appeared to give relief, but as there were only small quantities available, the relief was only temporary.

I beg to make the following recommendations:
(1) Extra stretchers and bearers should at once be sent up from Field Ambulances to remove men affected as soon as possible. This would prevent men trying to walk

back, and would prevent men lying in the sun.

(2) Large quantities of ammonia should be sent up to the trenches whenever there is a gas alert.

(3) All methods of treating cases should be very easily got at when there is a chance of a gas attack. For instance there should be an oxygen apparatus at the Advanced Dressing Station, if not actually in the front line trench.

(4) There are not sufficient Vermorel Sprayers at present on charge.

(5) Men affected have a great tendency to wish to hide in dug-outs. Stringent steps should be taken to prevent this.

(6) At the time of a gas alert the actual number of men in the firing line should be reduced to an absolute minimum compatible with safety. The defence of the line could well be trusted largely to Machine and Lewis guns. There were practically no cases of men in the back lines being affected. Those that were, were only slightly so.

Signed: D. E. Cayley,
Brigadier-General,
Commanding 88th Infantry Brigade.

Further Report on German Gas Attack on night 8/9 August, 1916

(1) It is doubtful if the helmets were entirely effective. There were several cases of men gassed with helmets on. Possibly this arose from the greater strength of the gas, or to the presence of some new constituent. Men who were affected later on may have absorbed the poison while their helmets were on, the effects of the poison not declaring itself till an interval had elapsed.

The P.G.H. helmet was criticized by some wearers, as owing to the sponge eye-pieces it was not possible to rub the inside of the eye-pieces against the forehead and so clear off the vapour.

(2) The box respirators appear to have been satisfactory. Of three Lewis gunners who wore them in the front line, two were completely immune.

(3) No complaints that P.G.H. helmets took longer to put on. Everyone had plenty of time to adjust his helmet properly.

(4) Vermorel Sprayers were used. There should be more of these on charge. They were effective as regards the chlorine, though it is impossible to say how far they cleared the phosgene out; which I understand to be a tasteless and odourless gas.

(5) There are very few real dug-outs in the part of my line affected, most of these being in the form of shelters without gas protection. The protection afforded appears to have been adequate, as officers were able to telephone without bad results. I attach a report from Officer Commanding 2nd Hampshire Regiment. This seems to make it quite clear that the casualties were not caused by the removal of helmets too soon, but that the helmets were not a sufficient protection.

Signed: D. E. Cayley.
12.8.16.

To 88th Brigade

Reference to German Gas Attack on the night of 8th instant. On the night in question two platoons (strength 1 Officer and 43 other ranks) were working in the Gully in rear of the right firing line Company and on the right of the gas area. On receiving the alarm these 2 platoons put on their helmets and remained still. After the cloud had passed they moved up to the firing line and manned the trench over which the main cloud had passed. They took off their helmets when the right Company removed theirs. After about twenty minutes the men of the Company began to feel ill and many died, while in the two platoons there were only 2 casualties which were caused through faults of the individuals concerned.

With the left firing line Company there was another platoon of the support Company. This platoon was up in the front trench when the gas came over and was all gassed except the platoon officer and 1 man.

It appears from the above, either that the gas cloud was too strong for the helmets or that the helmets were not proof against one of the gases used.

The case of the two platoons clears up any doubt of the helmets being removed too soon.

(Sgd) W. H. Middleton, Lt. Colonel,
Commanding 2nd/Hampshire Regiment
12.8.16

The Regimental Diary records the happenings of that night as follows:

August 8th 1916
On the night of 8th/9th the gas alarm was sounded by the horn on our left. The wind was from the NE and very light and as soon as the gas cloud was observed to be approaching our line the alarm was taken up and due precautions made. The cloud took about one hour to pass and came in two waves. During this time our supporting artillery opened a barrage of shrapnel fire and the enemy made no attempt to leave his trenches. The enemy at the same time opened a fairly heavy shrapnel fire on to our front line system and main communications. A few large howitzer shells being directed at our reserves. The gas seemed to be of a particularly deadly kind and penetrated a considerable distance, the effect being felt some distance in rear. It was noticeable that the gas corroded all metal that it came in contact with and killed many rats and birds.

Casualties. Capt. P. B. S. Hall, Lieut. E. W. C. Turner, 2/Lt. H. C. Scoggin, 2/Lt. J. McCurdy (killed), 2/Lts. G. A. Millet, A. W. H. Foster, M. T. Smith, L. H. Churcher, M. C. Tollemache, J. Graham.

O.Rs. 125 killed (and died of wounds), 100 wounded. On the night of 9th/10th Bn. was relieved by the 1st/Essex Regiment.

The repercussions from that night rippled upwards and caused a flutter in some quite highly placed dovecotes. Here are the comments from the diary of Brigade Headquarters:

Ypres 8th August The Germans let off gas at about ten-forty p.m. Everything was in order and the men had got their helmets on by the time the gas-cloud came over. Notwithstanding this the Hampshire Regiment suffered severe casualties, about 215 in all, from gas. The gas appears to have been let off a little bit to the North of us. The Royal Inniskilling Fusiliers, like the Hampshire Regiment, suffered heavy casualties, but the Worcestershire Regiment suffered no casualties. Gas was distinctly smelt both at Hampshire Regiment's H.Q., and at Worcestershire H.Q. This goes to show that gas was let off diagonally across our front. No infantry attack followed.

August 9th Enquiries set on foot regarding the number of casualties in last night's Gas Attack. From these, it appears evident that there was no question of the men in the Hampshire Regiment being surprised without their helmets; every man had plenty of time to put on his helmet, and in one case a Company Commander actually inspected the helmets to ensure that they were properly fastened and put on. A great many men who had apparently been slightly gassed walked from the firing line to the Dressing Station, where they collapsed and died. Further orders have been issued about the action of men to be taken in the case of gas etc., the chief of these being that during a Gas Alert parties of men within 1,000 yards of the enemy are to wear their helmets in the Gas Alert position. Men who have been slightly gassed are, on no account, to be allowed to walk down to the Dressing Station, but must remain where they are, as quiet as possible, until they are carried down thus avoiding the extra exertion which appears to be fatal in these cases.

August 10th The Corps Commander and the Divisional Commander visited Brigade H.Q. where they met General Cayley and General Lucas and enquired into the details of the Gas Attack.

These enquiries resulted in the two official reports quoted above. No one asked Private Byrne for his version of the affair, but on one matter at least, he and the high-ranking officers appear to agree – the helmets did not keep the gas out.

Appendix II

Military Organization

Below is listed the *nominal* basic structure of the British infantry during 1914–1918. These strengths varied a good deal during the war, however; in 1918, for example, they were considerably reduced.

Section = 12–15 men, plus an NCO

4 sections = 1 platoon

4 platoons = 1 company

4 companies = 1 battalion (30 officers, 992 ORs plus 1 doctor, 24 bandsmen/stretcher-bearers, 1 Quartermaster and 30 transport drivers, clerks, cooks, tailors, storemen etc.)

4 battalions = 1 brigade (plus brigade troops, i.e. field artillery, field ambulance unit, signals, engineers etc.)

3 brigades = 1 division (18,073 all ranks including divisional troops, 76 guns and 24 machine-guns. Marching depth about 15 miles)

3 or 4 divisions = 1 army corps

Variable number of corps (5 on the Somme in 1916) = 1 army. Ultimately, there were 5 British armies under the command of General Sir Douglas (later

Field-Marshal Earl) Haig, the Commander-in-Chief from 1915.

The most important unit with which the ordinary infantryman identified was the battalion — the 2nd Hampshires, in Charlie Byrne's case, although special circumstances were to tie him closely to the 1st Newfoundland Regiment. Beyond that, soldiers tended to be aware of their divisions. In Private Byrne's case, this was the 29th (Infantry) Division, comprising 86, 87 and 88 Brigades. Each man wore upon his shoulder a cloth patch indicating the division to which he belonged; 29th Division's was a narrow red triangle — half a diamond. This had been designed by the divisional commander, Major-General Sir H. de B. de Lisle, GOC from August 1915 to March 1918, to remind all ranks of the importance of the diamond formation in open fighting. The infantrymen, however, did not trouble themselves with such abstruse notions; all that they knew was that a man wearing the red triangular patches belonged to the same division as themselves, the 29th.

Nor was the slightly closer brigade formation of much concern to them. It is, however, as well to list them, as this gives an idea of the structure of a typical Regular infantry division of the mid-war period.

86 Brigade —
2nd Bn Royal Fusiliers
1st Bn Lancashire Fusiliers
1st Bn Royal Dublin Fusiliers
16th Bn Middlesex Regiment

87 Brigade —
2nd Bn South Wales Borderers
1st Bn King's Own Scottish Borderers
1st Bn Royal Inniskilling Fusiliers
1st Bn Border Regiment

88 Brigade —
4th Bn Worcestershire Regiment
1st Bn Essex Regiment
2nd Bn Hampshire Regiment
1st Bn Royal Newfoundland Regiment

Formed between January and March 1915, the 29th was the last of the old Regular Army divisions. The only 'amateur' soldiers in it were the Newfoundlanders, who had joined the division in Gallipoli in September 1915 to replace the 5th Bn the Royal Scots, which had sustained heavy losses there. In addition, on 22 May 1915 a troop train carrying two battalions of the Royal Scots from Larbert to Liverpool — presumably replacements for Gallipoli — crashed, in one of the worst railway disasters of all time, at Quintinshill, near the Scottish border. So the 1st Newfoundland Regiment joined 29th Division, and thus became briefly a part of Charlie Byrne's life — a part he never forgot.

The 29th, with the 4th, 31st and 48th Divisions, together made up VIII Corps, under Lieutenant-General Sir Aylmer Hunter-Weston. On the Somme, III, VIII, X, XIII and XV Corps comprised Fourth Army, commanded by General Sir Henry Rawlinson. All that, however, was a very long way indeed above Private Byrne's head.

Appendix III

The Battle of the Somme, July to November 1916

Below are listed the official names given to the twelve individual (though often overlapping) battles that collectively made up the Battle of the Somme.

Battle of Albert	1−13 July
Battle of Bazentin Ridge	13 July−3 September
Battle of Delville Wood	15 July−3 September
Battle of Pozières Ridge	23 July−3 September
Battle of Guillemont	3−6 September
Battle of Ginchy	9 September
Battle of Flers-Courcelette	15−22 September
Battle of Morval	25−28 September
Battle of Thiepval Ridge	26−28 September
Battle of the Transloy Ridges	1−18 October
Battle of the Ancre Heights	1 October−11 November
Battle of the Ancre (1916)	13−18 November

Appendix IV

29th (Infantry) Division on the First Day on the Somme

Of the eighteen miles of front line along which the battle erupted that morning, 1 July 1916, only about one thousand yards, a little over half a mile, concerned Charlie Byrne and his unexpected comrades of the (Royal) Newfoundland Regiment. It is true that there was some success that day to the south, but, as Charlie points out in his narrative, there was none on the VIII Corps front.

The plans for the battle placed 88 Brigade in reserve, behind the 87th, which held the right of the corps frontage. 86 Brigade held the left, with the capture of Beaumont-Hamel village as their objective. 87 Brigade was assigned the task of capturing the German front line south of this, from the fortified village of Beaumont-Hamel roughly along Station Road. That achieved, they were then to proceed to their second objective, the capture of the German intermediate line on the Beaumont-Hamel–Beaucourt road. When all this had been accomplished, 88 Brigade was to pass through the other two brigades in a leap-frogging movement, and advance to capture Pusieux Trench, just beyond the Pusieux–Grandcourt road – a little under three miles from the start-line.

Facing 87 Brigade was a natural feature known to military history as 'Y Ravine', a very steep-sided cleft that began at the Ancre and ran to just south of Beaumont-Hamel itself. For the Germans, it was an excellent defensive position, and they had prudently sited their trenches just in front of it. In this sanctuary they had placed a number of machine-guns, which were to play an important part in the battle where the Newfoundlanders and Private Byrne were concerned.

The South Wales Borderers and the Inniskillings (87 Brigade) went over first. They were met with a storm of machine-gun fire that stopped most of them, literally, dead before they had even come through the gaps cut in their own wire. (Before the battle, gaps had been cut and marked in the British wire in front of the forward trenches to allow the passage of the assaulting troops. As one officer bitterly remarked, the advertisement of the attack was complete. The vital element of surprise was lacking, and it was little wonder that the Germans were able to direct their machine-guns with such fatal precision.) Those who survived the fire struggled past their dead and wounded comrades as best they could and formed up beyond the wire, inclined to the right according to orders, and moved out over No Man's Land at a slow walk.

A slow walk was all they could manage. In 1916, a British soldier went into battle with a minimum load of 66 pounds – nearly five extra stones in addition to his own weight. In 'fighting order' he carried a haversack containing shaving gear and extra socks, the unconsumed portion of the day's ration, special emergency rations, field dressings and iodine. He wore a heavy steel helmet, and carried a gas helmet and goggles, as well as rolled ground-sheet, water-bottle, entrenching tool, mess-tin, two sandbags, and 220 rounds of ammunition – and his rifle. Some of the rifles had wire-cutters attached to them. Most of the men carried items extra to this basic load: shovels, picks, wire, corkscrew stakes, extra bombs and ammunition, flares, and so on. Higher authority had considered every eventuality, but had missed one obvious point – a heavily laden man, however strong, is incapable of moving quickly. And slow-moving targets are very easy to hit. In addition to the machine-gun bullets, rifle and shell fire swept over the luckless South Wales Borderers and Inniskillings.

Five minutes later, the rest of the brigade, the King's Own Scottish Borderers and the Borders, climbed out of their trenches. They had in the interim been badly mauled by shell fire. With very few exceptions, this second wave did not even reach the swathes of dead and dying and wounded who marked the limit of the first wave's advance.

There then ensued a somewhat confused pause. Not in the machine-gun and rifle and shell fire — that went on — but in 87 Brigade's assault. Surely, now, someone in authority at the scene could have put a stop to the senseless carnage? But it was not that simple — nothing in that war ever was. For one thing, battles were cumbersome events involving thousands of men and hundreds of tons of munitions — once started, they tended to continue under the weight of their own momentum. Secondly, those in command received only very imperfect information, largely because of the communications problems that arose in such conditions and such terrain. In this case, the reports that came back tended to be encouraging, and thus misleading. It was stated — sincerely, though mistakenly — that some units had fought their way through to Station Road on the right, well behind the German front line. If this were so, they would have to be supported and reinforced before they were cut off.

At this point, there occurred a wry twist of fate. The whole story hinges on a coincidence, a tragic mistake involving a signalling flare. The prearranged signal that 87 Brigade had taken their first objective was the firing of a white flare. It was now reported to the divisional commander that white flares had been seen going up from 87 Brigade's right front. General de Lisle therefore ordered 88 Brigade to send two of its battalions into the attack, the other two being retained as divisional reserve. But white flares were also used by the Germans; in this case to indicate to their artillery that the guns were dropping rounds short. As the white flares soared into the blue sky, they beckoned the Newfoundlanders, to whom Charlie Byrne was (apparently unofficially) attached, on to the stage of history. It was nine-fifteen a.m., an hour and a quarter after the initial slaughter had begun, when the 1st Battalion the (Royal) Newfoundland Regiment went over the top. The other battalion ordered into the attack, the 1st Essex, had already been badly mauled by shell fire in the trenches, and could not even get started owing to the confusion and congestion caused by the wounded and the barrage. The reserve battalions − the 4th Worcesters and Charlie's own 2nd Hampshires − stood ready to repel any German counter-attacks that might materialize. Since they were now the only troops on the whole of 29th Division's front still in any sort of fighting shape, it is just as well that the expected counter-attack did not come. The Germans had also suffered heavily.

Three days later, on 4 July, VIII Corps came out of the line and was taken over by the Reserve Army (later renamed Fifth Army). So appalling were the corps' casualties on 1 July that neither it, nor 29th Division, took much further part in the Somme battles, which eventually petered out in freezing rain and mud in November.

Appendix V

Newfoundland Memorial Park, Beaumont-Hamel

29th Division never went back to Beaumont-Hamel, which was finally overrun by the 51st (Highland) Division in November 1916. They would not have recognized it even if they had done so. One military observer described the area as it was in May 1917: 'There is nothing to be seen of Beaumont-Hamel or Beaucourt. The whole ground is overlapping craters....' Still less would the men of the division have recognised the area in 1978, when Charlie Byrne made his only return trip to the Somme.

Shortly after the war, the Government of Newfoundland acquired in perpetuity the 84 acres of ground that was the sepulchre of so many of their dead. The repercussions of that day had been felt the length and breadth of the thinly populated island province; indeed, the shock-waves from the terrible result of 'The Great Drive for Beaumont-Hamel' (as they term it) are still felt today. For Newfoundlanders, no one else was there – it was their 'show', their glory, and their abiding grief. No one who can comprehend the sledge-hammer blows delivered to that tightly knit community by the losses of the First of July – least of all Charlie Byrne – would begrudge them their proprietorial rights to grief.

On the highest point they raised a mound of granite and clay, some 30 feet high, on which stands a colossal bronze caribou, the regimental emblem. It was cast by Basil Gotto, a well-known sculptor of the time, who gave it a noble head, surmounted by towering antlers and thrown back in an attitude despairingly defiant, its open mouth seemingly uttering some grievous, enquiring cry. Around the park's edges are planted evergreen trees from Newfoundland, and the wind, even on a quiet summer's day, never seems to cease its restless murmuring among them. For the rest, they left it exactly as they found it – shell-holes, trenches, corkscrew stakes and all – and allowed nature to clothe it with grass.

The idea that those 84 acres above Y Ravine would one day become a beautiful park, occupied by nothing more dangerous than visitors and gently grazing sheep, would have seemed very strange to the survivors of 29th Division as they marched away from the area on 25 July 1916.

Glossary

Technical terms and soldiers' slang as used by Private Byrne in the narrative.

Battle Order – reduced amount of infantry equipment: the pack was stored, and the haversack was moved into the place of the pack on the soldier's back. This was supposed to lighten the infantryman's load when he was going into battle, but as it was usually replaced by a still greater weight of spades, picks, bombs, sandbags, extra ammunition etc. it defeated the aim of making the soldier more mobile.

Bay – short for Fire Bay, which was that part of a fire trench which was manned. It usually had a fire-step, which was a ledge running along the forward side of a front-line trench, upon which soldiers stood to keep watch or to fire.

Blighty (noun) – England, home. Thought to be a corruption of a Hindustani word, *bilaik*, meaning a foreign country (to the Indians, especially England): it often occurred in the adjectival form *bilaiti*. The idea of home as a foreign country was an expression of the soldier's feeling that his civilian existence was so far removed from the ugly, insane, precarious nature of his Army life in 1914/1918 that it was like a remote foreign dream world. There was also a Persian word *vilayat*, that meant strange or foreign; and from this arose an Urdu corruption, *belait*, which soldiers distorted to Belati, and hence possibly Blighty. The Arabic word, *beladi*, 'my own country', is another possible source of derivation.

Blighty (adjective) – usually used of a wound, not fatal, but sufficiently serious to ensure that the recipient had to be sent to hospital in England ('a blighty one').

Bulling – inflicting pretentious nonsense and unnecessary ceremonial on the troops.

Chat – body louse: an insect, pale fawn in colour and of a creeping habit. It was almost impossible for a soldier, living in the same clothes for weeks on end and without bathing facilities, *not* to become 'chatty'. In quiet times or rest periods, sporadic attempts were made to be rid of these irritating parasites by running a thumb-nail up the seams of clothes, especially underwear, or by running a candle flame along the seams – this was known as 'chatting out'.

Chlorine – yellowish-green poison gas with a peculiarly irritating smell: attacked the lungs.

Coal-box – shell-burst of a 5.9 or heavier shell (so named from the big cloud of black smoke that arose on impact).

Dads – Cockney slang for feet.

Duckboard – device for flooring trenches or for making footpaths across boggy ground. It consisted of two narrow planks about eight feet long, across which were nailed horizontal slats about two feet wide. Very useful, but heavy to carry.

Dump – store for military requirements of all kinds; usually in the open behind the lines.

Enfilade – to sweep a trench from end to end with bullets and/or shells, bombs etc. from a position on the flank (to the side). This was an especial danger in salients (q.v.).

Eyes down, look in – phrase from the game of housey-housey (closely resembling modern bingo): meant everyone was settled down.

Fatigues – various chores and necessary jobs from

peeling potatoes to carrying ammunition, barbed wire, etc. up to the front line. Derivation obvious: the fighting soldier of the 1914/1918 War got little sleep and that mostly disturbed − this strain added to the humping of heavy loads ensured that he was tired out for most of the time.

Field Postcard − a stereotyped postcard on which various messages were printed, e.g. I am well: I have been wounded: I am going to the Base, etc. The soldier crossed out those that did not apply.

Five point nine − very destructive high-explosive shell. 5.9 is a translation to inches of 15 centimetres, which was the diameter (the calibre) of numerous German guns, at least a dozen models. The projectile weighed about 100lb.

GHQ − General Headquarters, i.e. the headquarters of the Commander-in-Chief. From 1916 onwards Sir Douglas Haig's headquarters were at Montreuil-sur-Mer.

Haversack − canvas bag containing a soldier's belongings, worn on the hip at the left (unless soldier was in Battle Order). Originally a trooper's bag for horse provender.

Jack Johnson − another nickname for a 5.9 shell burst which emitted clouds of black smoke. Jack Johnson was a famous black pugilist of the time. The other nickname for a 5.9 was a coal-box. (q.v).

Jankers − put in a military prison; often applied to all sorts of military punishments.

Kilo − short for kilometre (5/8 of an English mile).

Knew his bill − knew what to do.

Limber − detachable wheeled part of a gun-carriage, used for transporting a number of different military stores.

MG − Machine-gun.

Over the top/bags/plonk − in order to make an assault

the troops had to hoist themselves out of the sheltering trench and over the parapet — the front wall of sandbags. The rearward side of the trench was known as the parados.

PBI — Poor bloody infantry.

p.d.q. pretty damned quick.

PH or tube helmet — protection from gas: head covering made from standard grey flannel Army shirt material. It had mica eye-pieces and a rubber-tipped metal tube to be held between the teeth for exhalation. (P stands for phenol, carbolic acid with which the flannel was impregnated.)

PHG — an improvement on the PH helmet, made from heavier flannel. The eye-pieces were made of glass and had sponge rubber round them which fitted close to the cheek. Both helmets were generally referred to as gas-bags, gas helmets or gas-masks. They were superseded in 1917 by the more efficient box respirator.

Phosgene — poison gas, lethal even in small doses.

Pop — short for Poperinghe, small town west of Ypres.

Puttee — khaki cloth band wound round the leg from the top of the boot to just below the knee; designed to give support when marching. (Derived from the Hindustani word for bandage.)

Red-caps — Military Police. They wore a red flannel cover over the top of their khaki caps. Not a popular military species.

Regimental number — identification number given to a man upon enlistment and kept throughout his service career.

Ruti — Hindi word for bread, now usually spelled 'roti'.

Salient — part of a trench system jutting out towards the enemy's line.

The Salient — the trench lines outside Ypres to the east. Salients were always dangerous places to inhabit, but this particular one was peculiarly unhealthy because not only did the enemy form a semi-circle, thus enabling men to be shot at from most directions, but they occupied higher ground and could see clearly what was going on in the British lines.

Sap — a sort of trench; but a trench was made by digging downwards, a sap was made by digging outwards from an existing trench. A Russian sap was a trench dug in the direction of the enemy lines but with a roof, usually of earth, to camouflage it. Russian saps were normally temporary, used for assembly before an attack.

Stamping his feet on parade — drawing attention to himself (very unpopular).

Transport lines — the base from which material was moved forward by wheeled transport or mules; as close to the front line as practicable.

Traverse (noun) — partitions (in trenches) built of sandbags: their purpose was to prevent enfilade fire (q.v.) and to confine the effects of bursting shells and bombs.

Traversing (verb) — a machine-gun's pivot through an arc, sweeping a fan of bullets ahead.

u/s — unserviceable, useless.

Vermorel sprayer — resembled a garden insecticide sprayer; was filled with chemicals designed to disperse gas clouds that hung low on the ground and in trenches after a gas attack.

Very light — (pronounced Veery) cartridge containing a flare which was fired from a brass pistol. Brass was an expensive metal, but Very lights were trench stores and brass does not rust nor corrode so easily when stored in damp places. The Very lights were used to illuminate No Man's Land at night; they gave a brilliant blue-white light that lasted for several seconds. Also used for signalling.

Webbing – khaki equipment made out of coarse canvas cloth; formed straps and so on, upon which items were buckled.

Wiring party – squad detailed to put up defensive entanglements of barbed wire in front of a trench. Almost always this was done at night: it was a dangerous and unpopular task.

Ypres – small town in north-west Belgium. In 1914/early 1915 it seems to have been pronounced 'Wipers' by British troops. But Charlie called it 'Eepray'.

BIBLIOGRAPHY

Banks, Arthur, *A Military Atlas of the First World War*, Heinemann, 1975

Brophy, John, and Partridge, Eric, *The Long Trail*, Deutsch, 1965

Brown, Malcolm, *The Imperial War Museum Book of the First World War*, Sidgwick & Jackson, 1991

---, *Tommy Goes To War*, Dent, 1978

Cave, Joy B., *Two Newfoundland VCs*, Creative Printers, 1984

---, *What Became of Corporal Pittman?*, Breakwater, 1974

Coombs, Rose E. B., *Before Endeavours Fade*, Battle of Britain Prints International, 1976

de Watteville, Colonel H., *The British Soldier*, Dent, 1954

Doyle, Sir Arthur Conan, *The British Campaigns in France and Flanders 1916*, Hodder & Stoughton, 1918

Edmonds, Brigadier-General Sir J. E. (ed.), *History of the Great War: Military Operations, France and Belgium 1916* (Official History), Macmillan and HMSO, 1932

Farrar-Hockley, A. H., *The Somme*, Batsford, 1964

Gardner, R. B., *The Big Push*, Cassell, 1961

Gillon, Captain Stair, *History of the 29th Division*, Nelson, 1925

Gliddon, Gerald, *When The Barrage Lifts*, Gliddon Books, 1987

Hammerton, Sir J. A. (ed.), *A Popular History of the Great War*, III, *The Allies at Bay*, Amalgamated Press, n.d.

Harris, John, *The Somme: Death of a Generation*, Hodder & Stoughton, 1966

Masefield, John, *The Old Front Line*, 1917, reprinted Spur Books, 1972

Maurice, Major-General Sir Frederick, *The Last Four Months*, Cassell, 1919

Monthly Army List: March 1916, HMSO

Nicholson, Colonel G. W. L., *The Fighting Newfoundlander*, Government of Newfoundland, 1964

Walsh, Colin (comp.), *Mud, Songs and Blighty*, Hutchinson, 1975